THE COMPLETE FOODI 2-BASKET AIR FRYER COOKBOOK 2021

Easy, Tasty, Delicious Recipes for Beginners and Advanced Users to Enjoy Easier, Healthier, & Crispier Foods.

PATY BREADS

PATY BREADS

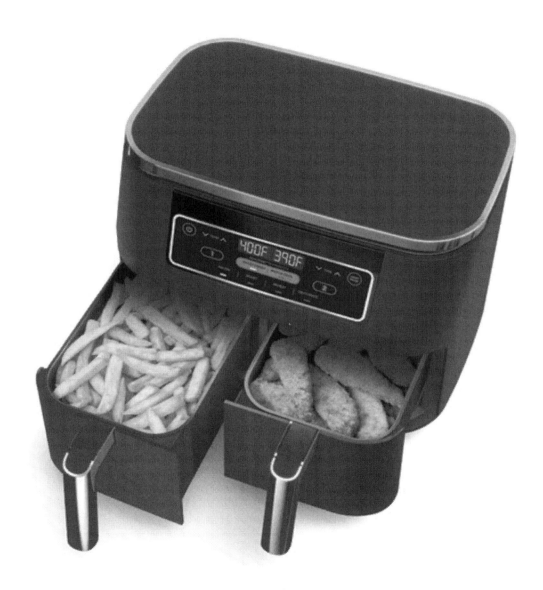

© Copyright 2021 - All rights reserved.

Table of Contents

Introduction

The Foodi 2-Basket Air Fryer is an appliance with a lot of good features. It's one of the most popular Air Fryers on the market today, and it's affordable. The Foodi 2-Basket Air Fryer offers a lot of great features including a touchscreen display, adjustable temperature, and a digital timer. It's also easy to clean with non-stick surfaces and dishwashable baskets.

Now you can get the same delicious fried food that comes from fried food restaurants, without the grease, saturated fats, and calories that come from cooking in oil. The Foodi 2-Basket Air Fryer uses 100% air technology to cook your food, so there's no need to use oil at all. The Foodi 2-Basket Air Fryer offers a couple of different baskets to help you cook different types of foods at once. The larger basket allows you to fry larger cuts of meat and the smaller basket is great for things like fries and wings. Air Fryers are currently the real deal. If you've been wanting to try one out then we have the perfect product for you: The Foodi 2-Basket Air Fryer. This nifty little gadget can air fry, steam, grill, roast, and bake.

At its heart, the Foodi 2-Basket Air Fryer is a simple and exceedingly effective Air Fryer that gives you all the basic functions that you would expect from an Air Fryer. With this appliance, you can air fry, bake, broil, dehydrate, air crisp, and more! You know, the usual Air Fryer stuffs.

However, it is the dual-zone technology that completely flips the game in the air frying market.

If you wish to reduce your cooking to half, or you want to make two different meals at the same time, in the same appliance, then the Foodi Dual-Zone/2-Basket Air Fryer is exactly what you need! In a simple way, the dual-zone technology allows the appliance to be put on either Single Cook mode or Multi Cook mode.

Single Cook mode works as usual; you cook using just a single basket. However, with the Multi Cook mode, you can seamlessly set the different timer, mode, and temperature for both of the zones individually and cook the meals you require.

Alternatively, you may give the same settings to both of the zones and cook the same meal in a doubled portion without spending any more time than you would need when making just a single portion. While handling two Air Fryer baskets might sound a little bit complicated at first, the way how Kitchen has engineered this appliance has made it extremely accessible and easy to handle. This appliance is extremely awesome for people who love the bake and cook crispy foods.

This particular Air Fryer comes with 2 different fryer baskets, which are marked as 1 and 2. Each should be inserted into their respective section of the appliance because of their different shapes.

Keep in mind that the baskets themselves don't have any buttons, so you can just pull them out and insert them as needed.

The display itself is divided into 2 different sections that indicate each section of the Basket settings. Pres "Key 1" on the control panel to select basket 1 setting and "Key 2" for basket 2 settings.

CHAPTER 1:

Introduction to 2-Basket Air Fryer

The Foodi 2-Basket Air Fryer is a new arrival amongst the wide range of Air Fryers. This Air Fryer has 2 independent baskets that let you cook two different food items or bulk of food at the same time with two different or the same settings. It is way different than the traditional Air Fryer that usually has a single basket.

As by the name, this comprehensive guide is targeted toward all those busy people who want to enjoy some delicious but less fatty meal that tastes delicious and its texture is as crispy as restaurant meals.

So, if you are a housewife or have an on-to-go lifestyle, then this Foodi is an excellent appliance to fulfill all your cooking needs. Whether it's an early morning breakfast, afternoon brunch, or late-night dinner party, now you can create some remarkable restaurant-style meals right in your kitchen. Take advantage of any of the recipes provided in this cookbook to enjoy a meal that keeps your weight maintained.

The Foodi 2-Basket Air Fryer lets you prepare food that is delicious and offers a hand-free cooking experience with less hustle. This cookbook includes easily prepared meals targeted toward the American audience.

No doubt, the Foodie 2-Basket Air Fryer plays a very important role in making healthy meals. Unlike any other appliance like a deep fryer and broiler, it prepares food in less oil. Now, stop sacrificing the taste and texture and enjoy whatever you like.

The new Foodie 2-Basket Air Fryer has a dual-zone technology that includes a smart finish button that cooks two food items in two different ways at the same time. It has a "Match" button that cooks food by copying the setting across both zones.

The 8-quart Air Fryer has a capacity that can cook full family meals up to 4 pounds. The two zones have their separate baskets that cook food using cyclonic fans that heat food rapidly with circulating hot air all-around. The baskets are very easy to clean and dishwasher safe. The Foodi 2-Basket Air Fryer has a range of 105–450°F temperature.

The Foodi 2-Basket Air Fryer is easily available at an affordable price online and at local stores.

If you are always worried about the lack of time to prepare two different meals or a large number of meals in a single go, then this appliance is a must-have.

The Functions of Foodi 2-Basket Air Fryer

This Foodie 2-Basket Air Fryer eliminates the traditional back-to-back cooking by providing ease of two baskets that cook food at the same time.

Its functions include a Smart Finish feature cooking system, so both items of food are cooked at the same time.

This Foodi Air Fryer surely makes crispy food by removing the moist from the food by circulating the hot air around.

The Air Fryer function includes:

- Air fry
- Air broil
- Roast
- Bake
- Reheat
- Dehydrate

Item weight: 24.3 pounds

Manufacturer: Kitchen

If you want to end the cooking time of one zone, while using both zones you need to choose the zone you like to stop, and then press the "Start/Stop" button to end the cooking process for that specific zone.

When the drawer is removed from the Foodi 2-Basket Air Fryer, the cooking process is automatically stopped.

The "Temp" arrows are used to set the desired temperature.

The "Time" arrows are used to set the time according to specific needs.

Once cooking is done, "End" will appear on the screen.

CHAPTER 2:

Advantages of Having 2 Baskets Instead of 1

The 2-Basket Air Fryer is known for several of its advanced features and its ultimate benefits.

Smart Finish

This cooking miracle can intelligently sync the cook times of both the cooking zones so that you cook different foods at a time with the same finishing time. So, here is how it works! When you add different food to the two baskets, and each has its own cooking time. When you cook using the Smart Cooking function and start the operation, the basket with the longer cooking time will initiate its operation first while the other basket will stay on hold until the other chamber reaches the same cooking time. In this way, both sides finish cooking at the same time.

Match Cook

The total 8-quart capacity of this Air Fryer is divided into two 4-quart Air Fryer baskets, which means that you get to cook different food and the same food in the two baskets at a time. Using the match cook technology, you can use the same cooking function for both the baskets and use its XL capacity.

XL 8-Quart Capacity

The large 8-quart capacity divide into two parts gives you a perfect space to cook food in a large and small amount. This capacity is enough to cook 2 lbs. of fries and 2 lbs. of wings and drumettes.

Nonstick for Easy Cleaning

Both baskets are nonstick, so they are easy to clean and wash. Crisper plates that are lined at the base of the baskets are dishwasher safe so you can wash them without damaging them.

Structural Composition of the Foodi Dual-Zone Air Fryer

The Digital Foodi Air Fryer has brought such a revolution into the kitchen that now the users can enjoy fresh and crispy meals in no time.

The control panel is present right on top of the basket's inlets, and it covers the front top portion of the Air Fryer. The top of the Air Fryer unit is flat, and it does not produce much heat. Do not place anything on the flat top of the Air Fryer unit or nearby. The control panel is designed with functions and operating buttons.

The display screen is divided into two sections, each indicating the cooking status of its side of the basket. To select the settings for basket 1, press "Key 1" on the control panel, and to select the settings for basket 2, press "Key 2" on the control. The other functions and operating keys include:

Function Buttons
- **Air broil:** This mode gives a crispy touch to the meals and you can use it to melt the toppings of the food.
- **Air fry:** Cook crispy fried food without the use of oil with the help of this mode.
- **Roast:** Turn this Air Fryer unit into a roaster oven to cook soft and tender meat.
- **Bake:** Cook delicious baked desserts and treats.
- **Reheat:** Allow you to reheat and warm your leftovers meals.
- **Dehydrate:** Use this mode to dehydrate fruits, meats, and vegetables.

Operating Buttons
- **Temp keys:** The up and down key allows you to adjust the cooking temperature.
- **Time arrows:** The up and down keys are there to adjust the cooking time.
- **"Smart Finish" button:** This mode automatically syncs the cooking times of both of the cooking zones and lets them finish at the same time.
- **"Match Cook" button:** Allows you to automatically match the settings of zone 2 to those of the cooking zone 1, which lets you cook a larger amount of the same food or different type of food in the same settings.
- **"Start/Pause" button:** These buttons are used to initiate, stop, and resume the cooking.
- **Power button:** The button is pressed to turn on or off the unit once the cooking function is completedd or stopped.
- **Standby mode:** In this mode, the Power button will get dimly lit, and the machine goes into standby if there is no activity for 10 minutes.
- **Hold mode:** The hold sign will appear on the display screen when it is in the Smart Finish mode. When the cooking time of one zone is greater than the other, then the hold will appear for the zone with less cooking time until its cooking time matches with the other one.

The Dual-Zone Technology

The amazing dual-zone technology of the Air Fryer will let you cook using the following two modes:

Smart Finish Technology

This function is used to finish cooking at the same time when foods in the 2 Air Fryer baskets have different cook temps, times, or even cooking functions. To do so, you only have to follow the next steps:

1. Add all the ingredients into the baskets, then insert baskets in the Air Fryer unit.
2. Press the Smart Finish mode, and the machine will automatically sync during cooking.
3. At first, zone 1 will stay illuminated. Now select the cooking function for this zone. Use the Temp key to set the required temperature, and use the Time keys to set the required time.
4. Now select zone 2, and select the cooking function.
5. Use the Temp keys to set the temperature, then use the Time key to set the time for zone 2.

6. Press the "Start" button, and the timer will start ticking for both zones according to their timings. And then, the cooking will be finished at the same time.
7. On Smart Finish mode, you can also start cooking at the same time and let it end at different times. For that, simply select their cooking time and press the "Start" button for both zones.

Match Cook

To cook a larger amount of the same food, or cook different foods using the same function, temperature, and time, you need to follow the next steps:

1. Add the cooking ingredients into the baskets, then insert both the baskets into the unit.
2. Zone 1 will stay illuminated. Press the desired function button. Use the Temp keys to set the cooking temperature, and use the Time keys to set the time.
3. Press the "Match Cook" button to copy the settings of basket 1 to basket 2.
4. Then press the "Start/Pause" button to Start cooking in both baskets.
5. Once the cooking is completedd "End" sign will appear on both screens.

CHAPTER 3:

Practical Tips and Smart Programs

To use the different cooking programs of the Foodi Air Fryer, you can try the following steps:

Air Broil

1. Insert crisper plate in the basket, then add ingredients into the basket, and insert basket in the unit.
2. The unit will default to zone 1, and to use zone 2 instead, select zone 2.
3. Select the Air Broil cooking mode.
4. Use the Temp keys to set the desired temperature.
5. Use the Time key to set the time from 1 minute to 1 hour and from 5 minutes to 1 or 4 hours.
6. Press the "Start/Pause" button to Start cooking.
7. The unit will beep once the cooking is completedd, and the "End" sign will appear on the display screen.
8. Remove ingredients from the basket by dumping them out onto the plate or using silicone utensils.

Air Fry

1. Insert crisper plate in the basket, then add ingredients into the basket, and insert basket in the unit.
2. The unit will default to zone 1, and to use basket 2 instead just select zone 2.
3. Select Air Fry cooking mode.
4. Use the Temp keys to set the required temperature.
5. Use the Time keys to set the time from 1 minute to 1 hour and from 5 minutes to 1 or 4 hours.
6. Press the "Start/Pause" button to Start cooking.
7. The unit will beep once the cooking is completedd, and the "End" sign will appear on display.

Bake

1. Insert crisper plate in the basket, then add ingredients into the basket, and insert basket in the unit.
2. Select Bake cooking mode.
3. Use the Temp keys to set the required temperature.
4. Use the Time keys to set the time in 1 minute increments up to 1 hour and in 5 minutes increments from 1 to 4 hours.

5. Press the "Start/Pause" button to begin cooking.
6. The unit will beep once the cooking is completedd, and the "End" sign will appear on the display screen.
7. Reduce the temperature by 25°F while converting the traditional oven recipes.

Other Cooking Modes

While using the other cooking modes, remember to follow the same steps, and select use the crisper plate or cooking rack as required. Then select the required mode, zone, and temperature then Start cooking. You can remove any of the baskets during the cooking process and shake the food inside, then reinsert the baskets to resume cooking. Press the "Start" button to resume cooking.

The broiling function is not available for the Match Cook technology; you can only broil the food in one basket at a time. If your food is in a large amount and you need to broil it, then broil in batches.

Tips on Good Use of Air Fryer

The use of Foodie 2-Basket Air Fryer is as easy as a click of a button.

For most of the recipes, it is necessary and recommended to grease the Air Fryer baskets with oil spray.

You simply add the food to the basket and select the required function to air fry, broil, bake, roast, and more.

The + and – buttons to adjust the cooking time and temperature control buttons can be separately used to adjust the cooking time of the food in both zones.

Once the food gets cooked, you can take out the baskets and serve food from both zones of the Air Fryer to the serving plates.

Some useful buttons to cook food:

- **Max crisp:** It is used to prepare some of the crispest French fries and chicken nuggets. With a lesser amount of oil, you can make more crispy food than a traditional fryer.
- **Roast:** The roast function easily prepares some tender and juicy meat in no time.
- **Reheat:** The reheat function can easily help you enjoy any leftover food.
- **Dehydrate:** Now you can easily dehydrate most of the fruits and the vegetables, and save money you spend to buy a separate dehydrator.
- **Bake:** This function helps creates delicious desserts and baked treats.
- **Sync button:** This button can be used when the user wants to finish two different zones with different settings together.
- **Match button:** This button automatically matches to both zones the time and the temperature.
- **Standby mode:** If the unit remains with no interaction for more than 10 minutes, it will go to standby mode.
- **Hold mode:** This will appear during sync mode, as one zone is cooking and the other is on hold.

Temperature Ranges

- **Bake function:** 250–400°F (Up to 1 ½ hour)

- **Roast function:** 250–400°F (For up to 4 hours)
- **Reheat function:** 270°F–400°F (1–60 minutes)
- **Dehydrate functions:** 105–195°F (1–12 hours)
- **Air broil function:** 400°F–450°F (1–30 minutes)

Maintaining and Cleaning the Appliance

- The 2-Basket Air Fryer is not intended to be used outdoor.
- It is very important to check the voltage indication are corresponding to the main voltage from the switch.
- Do not immerse the appliance in water.
- Keep the cord away from the hot area.
- Do not touch the outer surface of the Air Fryer hen using for cooking purposes.
- Put the appliance on a horizontal and flat surface.
- Unplug the appliance after use.

Cleaning and Maintenance

Here is how you can keep your 2-Basket Air Fryer clean and maintained after every session of cooking:

1. Unplug the appliance before cleaning it and allow it to cool completely.
2. You can remove the Air Fryer baskets from the main unit and keep them aside to cool.
3. Once cooled, remove their air crisper plates and wash them in the dishwasher.
4. Clean the Air Fryer basket using soapy water and avoid hard scrubbing to protect their nonstick layers.
5. Dishwash the Air Fryer racks in the dishwasher and use soft scrubs if the food is stuck to the rack.
6. Wipe the main unit with a clean piece of cloth or with a lightly damp cloth.
7. Once everything is cleaned and return the baskets to the Air Fryer.
8. Now your device is ready to use.

CHAPTER 4:

Breakfast

1. Turkey Morning Patties

Preparation time: 10 minutes
Cooking time: 13 minutes
Servings: 8
Ingredients

- 2 tsp. fennel seeds
- 1 lb. pork mince
- 2 tsp. dry rubbed sage
- 1 lb. turkey mince
- 2 tsp. garlic powder
- 1 tsp. paprika
- 1 tsp. sea salt
- 1 tsp. dried thyme

Directions

1. In a mixing bowl, add turkey and pork then mix them together.
2. Mix sage, fennel, paprika, salt, thyme, and garlic powder in a small bowl.
3. Drizzle this mixture over the meat mixture and mix well.
4. Take 2 tbsp. of this mixture at a time and roll it into thick patties.
5. Place half of the patties in basket 1 and the other half in basket 2 then spray them all with cooking oil.
6. Return the Air Fryer baskets to the Air Fryer.
7. Select the "Air Fryer" mode for Zone 1 with 390°F temperature and 13 minutes cooking time.
8. Press the "Match Cook" button to copy the settings for Zone 2.
9. Start cooking by pressing the "Start/Pause" button.
10. Flip the patties in the baskets once cooked halfway through.
11. Serve warm and fresh.

Nutrition

- Calories: 184
- Total fat: 7.9 g.
- Saturated fat: 1.4 g.
- Cholesterol: 36 mg.
- Sodium: 704 mg.
- Total carbohydrates: 6 g.
- Fiber: 3.6 g.
- Sugar: 5.5 g.
- Protein: 17.9 g.

2. Potato Hash Browns

Preparation time: 10 minutes
Cooking time: 13 minutes
Servings: 6
Ingredients

- 3 russet potatoes
- 2 garlic cloves chopped
- 1 tsp. paprika
- Black pepper to taste
- 2 tsp. olive oil

Directions

1. Peel and grate all the potatoes with a cheese grater.
2. Add potato shreds to a bowl filled with cold water and leave it soaked for 25 minutes.
3. Drain the water and place the potato shreds on a plate lined with a paper towel.
4. Transfer the shreds to a dry bowl and add olive oil, paprika, garlic, and black pepper.
5. Make 4 flat patties out of the potato mixture and place 2 into each of the Air Fryer baskets.
6. Return the Air Fryer baskets to the Air Fryer.
7. Select the "Air Fryer" mode for Zone 1 with 390°F temperature and 13 minutes cooking time.
8. Press the "Match Cook" button to copy the settings for Zone 2.
9. Start cooking by pressing the "Start/Pause" button.
10. Flip the potato hash browns once cooked halfway through, then resume cooking.
11. Once done, serve warm.

Nutrition

- Calories: 134
- Total fat: 4.7 g.
- Saturated fat: 0.6 g.
- Cholesterol: 124 mg.
- Sodium: 1 mg.
- Total carbohydrates: 54.1 g.
- Fiber: 7 g.
- Sugar: 3.3 g.
- Protein: 6.2 g.

3. Air Fried Breakfast Sausage

Preparation time: 10 minutes
Cooking time: 13 minutes
Servings: 4
Ingredients

- 4 sausage links, raw and uncooked

Directions

1. Divide the sausages into the 2 Air Fryer baskets.
2. Return the Air Fryer baskets to the Air Fryer.
3. Select the "Air Fryer" mode for Zone 1 with 390°F temperature and 13 minutes cooking time.
4. Press the "Match Cook" button to copy the settings for Zone 2.
5. Start cooking by pressing the "Start/Pause" button.
6. Serve warm and fresh.

Nutrition

- Calories: 187
- Total fat: 6 g.
- Saturated fat: 9.9 g.
- Cholesterol: 41 mg.
- Sodium: 154 mg.
- Total carbohydrates: 7.4 g.
- Fiber: 2.9 g.
- Sugar: 15.3 g.
- Protein: 24.6 g.

4. Egg Pepper Cups

Preparation time: 10 minutes
Cooking time: 12 minutes
Servings: 4
Ingredients

- 2 bell pepper, halved and seeds removed
- 8 eggs
- 1 tsp. olive oil
- 1 pinch salt and black pepper
- 1 pinch sriracha flakes

Directions

1. Slice the bell peppers in half, lengthwise, and remove their seeds and the inner portion to get a cup-like shape.
2. Rub olive oil on the edges of the bell peppers.
3. Place them in the 2 Air Fryer baskets with their cut side up and crack 2 eggs in each half of bell pepper.
4. Drizzle salt, black pepper, and sriracha flakes on top of the eggs.
5. Return the Air Fryer baskets to the Air Fryer.
6. Select the "Air Fryer" mode for Zone 1 with 390°F temperature and 18 minutes cooking time.
7. Press the "Match Cook" button to copy the settings for Zone 2.
8. Start cooking by pressing the "Start/Pause" button.
9. Serve warm and fresh.

Nutrition

- Calories: 212
- Total fat: 11.8 g.
- Saturated fat: 2.2 g.
- Cholesterol: 23 mg.
- Sodium: 321 mg.
- Total carbohydrates: 14.6 g.
- Dietary fiber: 4.4 g.
- Sugar: 8 g.
- Protein: 17.3 g.

5. Crispy Breakfast Bacon

Preparation time: 10 minutes

Cooking time: 14 minutes

Servings: 6

Ingredients

- ½ lb. bacon slices

Directions

1. Spread half of the bacon slices in each of the Air Fryer baskets evenly in a single layer.
2. Return the Air Fryer baskets to the Air Fryer.
3. Select the "Air Fryer" mode for Zone 1 with 390°F temperature and 14 minutes cooking time.
4. Press the "Match Cook" button to copy the settings for Zone 2.
5. Start cooking by pressing the "Start/Pause" button.
6. Flip the crispy bacon once cooked halfway through, then resume cooking.
7. Serve.

Nutrition

- Calories: 142
- Total fat: 24.8 g.
- Saturated fat: 12.4 g.
- Cholesterol: 3 mg.
- Sodium: 132 mg.
- Total carbohydrates: 0.8 g.
- Dietary fiber: 3.9 g.
- Sugar: 2.5 g.
- Protein: 18.9 g.

6. Egg Bacon Balls

Preparation time: 10 minutes
Cooking time: 14 minutes
Servings: 6
Ingredients

- 1 tbsp. butter
- 2 eggs, beaten
- ¼ tsp. pepper
- 1 can (10.2 oz) Pillsbury Buttermilk biscuits
- 2 oz Cheddar cheese, diced into 10 cubes
- Cooking spray
- Egg wash
- 1 egg
- 1 tbsp. water
- Bacon

Directions

1. Place a suitable non-stick skillet over medium-high heat and cook the bacon until crispy, then place it on a plate lined with a paper towel.
2. Melt butter in the same skillet over medium heat. Beat eggs with pepper in a bowl and pour them into the skillet.
3. Stir cook for 5 minutes then remove it from the heat.
4. Add bacon and mix well.
5. Divide the dough into 5 biscuits and slice each into 2 layers.
6. Press each biscuit into a 4-inch round.
7. Add a tbsp. of the egg mixture at the center of each round and top it with a piece of cheese.
8. Carefully fold the biscuit dough around the filling and pinch the edges to seal.
9. Whisk egg with water in a small bowl and brush the egg wash over the biscuits.
10. Place half of the biscuit bombs in each of the Air Fryer baskets and spray them with cooking oil.
11. Return the Air Fryer baskets to the Air Fryer.
12. Select the "Air Fryer" mode for Zone 1 with 375°F temperature and 14 minutes cooking time.
13. Press the "Match Cook" button to copy the settings for Zone 2.
14. Start cooking by pressing the "Start/Pause" button.
15. Flip the egg bombs when cooked halfway through, then resume cooking.
16. Serve warm.

Nutrition

- Calories: 331 Total fat: 2.5 g. Saturated fat: 0.5 g.
- Cholesterol: 35 mg. Sodium: 595 mg. Total carbohydrates: 29 g. Fiber: 12.2 g.
- Sugar: 12.5 g. Protein: 18.7 g.

7. Crispy Egg Rolls

Preparation time: 10 minutes
Cooking time: 13 minutes
Servings: 6
Ingredients

- 2 eggs
- 2 tbsp. milk
- Salt to taste
- Black pepper to taste
- ½ c. shredded Cheddar cheese
- 2 sausage patties
- 6 egg roll wrappers
- 1 tbsp. olive oil
- 1 c. water

Directions

1. Grease a small skillet with some olive oil and place it over medium heat.
2. Add sausage patties and cook them until brown.
3. Chop the cooked patties into small pieces. Beat eggs with salt, black pepper, and milk in a mixing bowl.
4. Grease the same skillet with 1 tsp. olive oil and pour the egg mixture into it.
5. Stir cook to make scrambled eggs.
6. Add sausage, mix well and remove the skillet from the heat.
7. Spread an egg roll wrapper on the working surface in a diamond shape position.
8. Add a tbsp. cheese at the bottom third of the roll wrapper.
9. Top the cheese with the egg mixture and wet the edges of the wrapper with water.
10. Fold the 2 corners of the wrapper and roll it, then seal the edges.
11. Repeat the same steps and divide the rolls into the 2 Air Fryer baskets.
12. Return the Air Fryer baskets to the Air Fryer.
13. Select the "Air Fryer" mode for Zone 1 with 375°F temperature and 13 minutes cooking time.
14. Press the "Match Cook" button to copy the settings for Zone 2.
15. Start cooking by pressing the "Start/Pause" button.
16. Flip the rolls after 8 minutes and continue cooking for another 5 minutes.
17. Serve warm and fresh.

Nutrition

- Calories: 322 Total fat: 11.8 g.
- Saturated fat: 2.2 g. Cholesterol: 56 mg.
- Sodium: 321 mg.Total carbohydrates: 14.6 g.
- Dietary fiber: 4.4 g.Sugar: 8 g. Protein: 17.3 g.

8. Spinach Egg Cups

Preparation time: 10 minutes
Cooking time: 13 minutes
Servings: 4
Ingredients

- 4 tbsp. milk
- 4 tbsp. frozen spinach, thawed
- 4 large egg
- 8 tsp. grated cheese
- Salt to taste
- Black pepper to taste
- Cooking spray

Directions

1. Grease 4 small-sized ramekin with cooking spray.
2. Add egg, cheese, spinach, and milk to a bowl and beat well.
3. Divide the mixture into 4 small ramekins and top them with salt and black pepper.
4. Place the 2 ramekins in each of the 2 Air Fryer baskets.
5. Return the Air Fryer baskets to the Air Fryer.
6. Select the "Air Fryer" mode for Zone 1 with 390°F temperature and 13 minutes cooking time.
7. Press the "Match Cook" button to copy the settings for Zone 2.
8. Start cooking by pressing the "Start/Pause" button.
9. Serve warm.

Nutrition

- Calories: 197
- Total fat: 15.4 g.
- Saturated fat: 4.2 g.
- Cholesterol: 168 mg.
- Sodium: 203 mg.
- Total carbohydrates: 8.5 g.
- Sugar: 1.1 g.
- Fiber: 4 g.
- Protein: 17.9 g.

9. Pumpkin Muffins

Preparation time: 10 minutes
Cooking time: 13 minutes
Servings: 6
Ingredients

- ½ cup pumpkin puree
- 1 cup gluten-free oats
- ¼ cup honey
- 1 medium egg beaten
- ½ tsp. coconut butter
- ½ tbsp. cocoa nib
- ½ tbsp. vanilla essence
- Cooking spray
- ½ tsp. nutmeg

Directions

1. Add oats, honey, egg, pumpkin puree, coconut butter, cocoa nibs, vanilla essence, and nutmeg to a bowl and mix well until smooth.
2. Divide the batter into 2 4-cup muffin trays, greased with cooking spray.
3. Place one mini muffin tray in each of the 2 Air Fryer baskets.
4. Return the Air Fryer baskets to the Air Fryer.
5. Select the "Air Fryer" mode for Zone 1 with 375°F temperature and 13 minutes cooking time.
6. Press the "Match Cook" button to copy the settings for Zone 2.
7. Start cooking by pressing the "Start/Pause" button.
8. Allow the muffins to cool then serve.

Nutrition

- Calories: 138
- Total fat: 9.7 g.
- Saturated fat: 4.7 g.
- Cholesterol: 181 mg.
- Sodium: 245 mg.
- Total carbohydrates: 32.5 g.
- Fiber: 0.3 g.
- Sugar: 1.8 g.
- Protein: 10.3 g.

10.French Toast Sticks

Preparation time: 10 minutes
Cooking time: 8 minutes
Servings: 2
Ingredients

- 4 pieces of bread
- 2 tbsp. butter
- 2 eggs, beaten
- 1 pinch salt
- 1 pinch cinnamon ground
- 1 pinch nutmeg ground
- 1 pinch ground clove

Directions

1. Add 2 eggs to a mixing bowl and stir cinnamon, nutmeg, ground cloves, and salt, then whisk well.
2. Spread butter on both sides of the bread slices and cut them into thick strips.
3. Dip the breadsticks in the egg mixture and place them in the 2 Air Fryer baskets.
4. Return the Air Fryer baskets to the Air Fryer.
5. Select the "Air Fryer" mode for Zone 1 with 390°F temperature and 8 minutes cooking time.
6. Press the "Match Cook" button to copy the settings for Zone 2.
7. Start cooking by pressing the "Start/Pause" button.
8. Flip the French toast sticks when cooked halfway through.
9. Serve.

Nutrition

- Calories: 391
- Total fat: 2.8 g.
- Saturated fat: 0.6 g.
- Cholesterol: 330 mg.
- Sodium: 62 mg.
- Total carbohydrates: 36.5 g.
- Fiber: 9.2 g.
- Sugar: 4.5 g.
- Protein: 6.6 g.

11. Breakfast Frittata

Preparation time: 35 minutes
Cooking time: 40 minutes
Servings: 2
Ingredients

- ¼ lb. breakfast sausage, cooked and crumbled
- 4 eggs, beaten
- ½ c. Cheddar cheese, shredded
- 1 red bell pepper, diced
- 1 green onion, chopped
- Cooking spray

Directions

1. Mix the eggs, sausage, cheese, onion, and bell pepper.
2. Spray a small baking pan with oil. Pour the egg mixture into the pan.
3. Set the basket inside. Close the Crisping Lid.
4. Choose the "Air Crisp" function. Cook at 360°F for 20 minutes.

Nutrition

- Calories: 380
- Total fat: 27.4 g.
- Saturated fat: 12.0 g.
- Cholesterol: 443 mg.
- Sodium: 694 mg.
- Total Carbohydrates 2.9 g.
- Dietary fiber: 0.4 g.
- Protein: 31.2 g.
- Sugar: 1 g.
- Potassium: 328 mg.

12.Egg in Toast

Preparation time: 15 minutes
Cooking time: 20 minutes
Servings: 1
Ingredients

- 1 slice bread
- 1 egg
- Salt and pepper to taste
- Cooking spray

Directions

1. Spray a small baking pan with oil. Place the bread inside the pan.
2. Make a hole in the middle of the bread slice.
3. Cracks open the egg and put it inside the hole.
4. Cover with the Crisping Lid. Set it to "Air Crisp."
5. Cook at 330°F for 6 minutes. Flip the toast and cook for 3 more minutes.

Nutrition

- Calories: 92
- Total fat: 5.2 g.
- Saturated fat: 1.5 g.
- Cholesterol: 164 mg.
- Sodium: 123 mg.
- Total carbohydrates: 5 g.
- Dietary fiber: 0.3 g.
- Total sugar: 0.7 g.
- Protein: 6.2 g.
- Potassium: 69 mg.

13.Baked Eggs

Preparation time: 10 minutes
Cooking time: 15 minutes
Servings: 1
Ingredients

- Cooking spray
- 1 egg
- 1 tsp. dried rosemary
- Salt and pepper to taste

Directions

1. Coat a ramekin with oil. Crack the egg into the ramekin.
2. Season with rosemary, salt, and pepper.
3. Close the Crisping Lid. Set it to "Air Crisp." Cook at 330°F for 5 minutes.

Nutrition

- Calories: 72
- Total fat: 5.1 g.
- Saturated fat: 1.5 g.
- Cholesterol: 164 mg.
- Sodium: 62 mg.
- Total carbohydrates: 1.2 g.
- Dietary fiber: 0.5 g.
- Total sugar: 0.3 g.
- Protein: 5.6 g.
- Potassium: 72 mg.

14. Breakfast Potatoes

Preparation time: 1 hour and 10 minutes
Cooking time: 1 hour and 20 minutes
Servings: 2
Ingredients

- 2 potatoes, scrubbed, rinsed, and diced
- 1 tbsp. olive oil
- Salt to taste
- ¼ tsp. garlic powder

Directions

1. Put the potatoes in a bowl of cold water. Soak for 45 minutes.
2. Pat the potatoes dry with a paper towel. Toss in olive oil, salt, and garlic powder.
3. Put in the basket. Seal the Crisping Lid. Set it to "Air Crisp."
4. Cook at 400°F for 20 minutes. Flip the potatoes halfway through.

Nutrition

- Calories: 208
- Total fat: 7.2 g.
- Saturated fat: 1.1 g.
- Cholesterol: 0 mg.
- Sodium: 90 mg.
- Total carbohydrates: 33.7 g.
- Dietary fiber: 5.1 g.
- Total sugar: 2.5 g.
- Protein: 3.6 g.
- Potassium: 871 mg.

15.Egg and Turkey Sausage Cups

Preparation time: 20 minutes
Cooking time: 25 minutes
Servings: 4
Ingredients

- 8 tbsps. turkey sausage, cooked and crumbled, divided
- 8 tbsps. frozen spinach, chopped and divided
- 8 tsps. shredded Cheddar cheese, divided
- 4 eggs

Directions

1. Add a layer of the sausage, spinach, and cheese on each muffin cup.
2. Crack the egg open on top. Seal the Crisping Lid. Set it to "Air Crisp."
3. Cook at 330°F for 10 minutes.

Nutrition

- Calories: 171
- Total fat: 13.3 g.
- Saturated fat: 4.7 g.
- Cholesterol: 190 mg.
- Sodium: 289 mg.
- Total carbohydrates: 0.5 g.
- Dietary fiber: 0.1 g.
- Total sugar: 0.4 g.
- Protein: 11.9 g.
- Potassium: 161 mg.

16. Omelets

Preparation time: 15 minutes

Cooking time: 20 minutes

Servings: 2

Ingredients

- 2 eggs
- ¼ c. milk
- 1 tbsp. red bell pepper, chopped
- 1 slice ham, diced
- 1 tbsp. mushrooms, chopped
- Salt to taste
- ¼ c. cheese, shredded

Directions

1. Whisk the eggs and milk in a bowl. Add the ham and vegetables. Season with salt.
2. Pour the mixture into a small pan. Place the pan inside the basket.
3. Seal the Crisping Lid. Set it to "Air Crisp." Cook at 350°F for 8 minutes.
4. Before it is fully cooked, sprinkle the cheese on top.

Nutrition

- Calories: 177
- Total fat: 11 g.
- Saturated fat: 5.1 g.
- Cholesterol: 189 mg.
- Sodium: 425 mg.
- Total carbohydrates: 7.1 g.
- Dietary fiber: 1 g.
- Total sugar: 4.8 g.
- Protein: 13.1 g.
- Potassium: 249 mg.

17.Cheesy Broccoli Quiche

Preparation time: 40 minutes
Cooking time: 45 minutes
Servings: 2
Ingredients

- 1 c. water
- 2 c. broccoli florets
- 1 carrot, chopped
- 1 c. Cheddar cheese, grated
- ¼ c. Feta cheese, crumbled
- 2 eggs
- 1 tsp. parsley
- 1 tsp. thyme
- Salt and pepper to taste

Directions

1. Pour the water inside. Place the basket inside.
2. Put the carrot and broccoli on the basket. Cover the pot.
3. Set it to "Pressure." Cook at high pressure for 2 minutes.
4. Release the pressure quickly. Crack the eggs into a bowl and beat.
5. Season with salt, pepper, parsley, and thyme. Put the vegetables on a small baking pan. Layer with the cheese and pour in the beaten eggs. Place on the basket.
6. Choose the "Air Crisp" function. Seal the Crisping Lid. Cook at 350°F for 20 minutes.

Nutrition

- Calories: 400
- Total fat: 28 g.
- Saturated fat: 16.5 g.
- Cholesterol: 242 mg.
- Sodium: 688 mg.
- Total carbohydrates: 12.8 g.
- Dietary fiber: 3.3 g.
- Total sugar: 5.8 g.
- Protein: 26.2 g.
- Potassium: 537 mg.

18.Bacon and Scrambled Eggs

Preparation time: 15 minutes
Cooking time: 20 minutes
Servings: 2
Ingredients

- 4 strips bacon
- 2 eggs
- 1 tbsp. milk
- Salt and pepper to taste

Directions

1. Place the bacon inside. Set it to "Air Crisp."
2. Cover the Crisping Lid. Cook at 390°F for 3 minutes.
3. Flip the bacon and cook for another 2 minutes. Remove the bacon and set it aside.
4. Whisk the eggs and milk in a bowl. Season with salt and pepper.
5. Set to sauté. Add the eggs and cook until firm.

Nutrition

- Calories: 272
- Total fat: 20.4 g.
- Saturated fat: 6.7 g.
- Cholesterol: 206 mg.
- Sodium: 943 mg.
- Total carbohydrates: 1.3 g.
- Dietary fiber: 0 g.
- Total sugar: 0.7 g.
- Protein: 19.9 g.
- Potassium: 279 mg.

19.French Toast

Preparation time: 15 minutes
Cooking time: 20 minutes
Servings: 2
Ingredients

- 2 eggs, beaten
- ¼ c. milk
- ¼ c. brown sugar
- 1 tbsp. honey
- 1 tsp. cinnamon
- ¼ tsp. nutmeg
- 4 slices wholemeal bread, sliced into strips

Directions

1. In a bowl, combine all the ingredients, except the bread. Mix well.
2. Dip each strip in the mixture. Place the bread strips on the basket.
3. Place basket inside the pot. Cover with the Crisping Lid. Set it to "Air Crisp."
4. Cook at 320°F for 10 minutes.

Nutrition

- Calories: 295
- Total fat: 6.1 g.
- Saturated fat: 2.1 g.
- Cholesterol: 166 mg.
- Sodium: 332 mg.
- Total carbohydrates: 49.8 g.
- Dietary fiber: 3.9 g.
- Total sugar: 29.4 g.
- Protein: 11.9 g.
- Potassium: 112 mg.

20. Eggs and Veggie Burrito

Preparation time: 30 minutes

Cooking time: 35 minutes
Servings: 8
Ingredients

- 3 eggs, beaten
- Salt and pepper to taste
- Cooking spray
- 8 tortillas
- 2 red bell peppers, sliced into strips
- 1 onion, sliced thinly

Directions

1. Beat the eggs in a bowl. Season with salt and pepper. Set aside.
2. Choose "Sauté" mode. Spray with the oil. Cook the vegetables until soft. Remove and set aside. Pour the eggs into the pot. Cook until firm.
3. Wrap the eggs and veggies with the tortillas.

Nutrition

- Calories: 92
- Total fat: 2.5 g.
- Saturated fat: 0.6 g.
- Cholesterol: 61 mg.
- Sodium: 35 mg.
- Total carbohydrates: 14.4 g.
- Dietary fiber: 2.2 g.
- Total sugar: 2.4 g.
- Protein: 3.9 g.
- Potassium: 143 mg.

21.Breakfast Casserole

Preparation time: 10 minutes
Cooking time: 20 minutes
Servings: 4
Ingredients

- Cooking spray
- 1 lb. hash browns
- 1 lb. breakfast sausage, cooked and crumbled
- 1 red bell pepper, diced
- 1 green bell pepper, diced
- 1 onion, diced
- 4 eggs
- Salt and pepper to taste

Directions

1. Coat a small baking pan with oil. Place the hash browns on the bottom part.
2. Add the sausage, and then the onion and bell peppers.
3. Place the pan on top of the basket. Put the basket inside the pot.
4. Close the Crisping Lid. Set it to "Air Crisp." Cook at 350°F for 10 minutes.
5. Open the lid. Crack the eggs on top. Cook for another 10 minutes.
6. Season with salt and pepper.

Nutrition

- Calories: 513
- Total fat: 34 g.
- Saturated fat: 9.3 g.
- Cholesterol: 173 mg.
- Sodium: 867 mg.
- Total carbohydrates: 30 g.
- Dietary fiber: 3.1 g.
- Total sugar: 3.1 g.
- Protein: 21.1 g.
- Potassium: 761 mg.

22.   Herb and Cheese Frittata

Preparation time: 25 minutes
Cooking time: 30 minutes
Servings: 4
Ingredients

- 4 eggs
- ½ c. half and half
- 2 tbsps. parsley, chopped
- 2 tbsps. chives, chopped
- ¼ c. shredded Cheddar cheese
- Salt and pepper to taste

Directions

1. Beat the eggs in a bowl. Add the rest of the ingredients and stir well.
2. Pour the mixture into a small baking pan.
3. Place the pan on top of the basket.
4. Seal the Crisping Lid. Set it to "Air Crisp." Cook at 330°F for 15 minutes.

Nutrition

- Calories: 132
- Total fat: 10.2 g.
- Saturated fat: 5 g.
- Cholesterol: 182 mg.
- Sodium: 119 mg.
- Total carbohydrates: 1.9 g.
- Dietary fiber: 0.1 g.
- Total sugar: 0.5 g.
- Protein: 8.3 g.
- Potassium: 121 mg.

23.   Roasted Garlic Potatoes

Preparation time: 15 minutes
Cooking time: 20 minutes
Servings: 6
Ingredients

- 2 lbs. baby potatoes, sliced into wedges
- 2 tbsps. olive oil
- 2 tsps. garlic salt

Directions

1. Toss the potatoes in olive oil and garlic salt.
2. Add the potatoes to the basket.
3. Seal the Crisping Lid.
4. Set it to "Air Crisp."
5. Cook at 390°F for 20 minutes.

Nutrition

- Calories: 131
- Total fat: 4.8 g.
- Saturated fat: 0.7 g.
- Cholesterol: 0 mg.
- Sodium: 15 mg.
- Total carbohydrates: 19.5 g.
- Dietary fiber: 3.9 g.
- Total sugar: 0.2 g.
- Protein: 4.1 g.
- Potassium: 635 mg.

24.   Tofu Scramble

Preparation time: 30 minutes
Cooking time: 35 minutes
Servings: 4
Ingredients

- 2 tbsps. olive oil, divided
- 2 tbsps. soy sauce
- ½ c. onion, chopped
- 1 tsp. turmeric
- ½ tsp. onion powder
- ½ tsp. garlic powder
- 1 block firm tofu, sliced into cubes

Directions

1. Mix all the ingredients except the tofu. Soak the tofu in the mixture.
2. Place the tofu in the pot. Seal the pot. Cover with the Crisping Lid.
3. Cook at 370°F for 15 minutes.

Nu0trition

- Calories: 90
- Total fat: 8 g.
- Saturated fat: 1.2 g.
- Cholesterol: 0 mg.
- Sodium: 455 mg.
- Total carbohydrates: 3.2 g.
- Dietary fiber: 0.7 g.
- Total sugar: 1.1 g.
- Protein: 2.7 g.
- Potassium: 93 mg.

25.   Avocado Egg

Preparation time: 10 minutes
Cooking time: 15 minutes
Servings: 2
Ingredients

- 1 avocado, sliced in half and pitted
- 2 eggs
- Salt and pepper to taste
- ¼ c. Cheddar, shredded

Directions

1. Crack the eggs into the avocado slices. Season with salt and pepper.
2. Put it on the basket. Seal the Crisping Lid.
3. Set it to "Air Crisp." Cook at 400°F for 15 minutes.
4. Sprinkle with the cheese 3 minutes before it is cooked.

Nutrition

- Calories: 281
- Total fat: 23 g.
- Saturated fat: 6 g.
- Cholesterol: 178 mg.
- Sodium: 158 mg.
- Total Carbohydrates 9 g.
- Dietary fiber: 6 g.
- Protein: 11 g.
- Potassium: 548 mg.

26.   Homemade Yogurt

Preparation time: 15 minutes
Cooking time: 12 hours
Servings: 8
Ingredients

- ½ gallon whole milk
- 2 tbsps. plain yogurt with active live cultures
- 1 tbsp. vanilla extract (optional)
- ½ c. honey (optional)

Directions

1. Pour the milk into the pot. Assemble the Pressure Lid, making sure the pressure release valve is in the "Vent" position. Select "Sear/Sauté" and set it to Medium. Select "Start/Stop" to begin.
2. Bring the milk to 180°F, checking the temperature often and stirring frequently so the milk does not burn at the bottom. Select "Start/Stop" to turn off "Sear/Sauté."
3. Allow the milk to cool to 110°F, continuing to check the temperature often and stirring frequently. Gently skim off the "skin" on the milk and discard.
4. Stir in the yogurt and whisk until incorporated.
5. Assemble the Pressure Lid, making sure the pressure release valve is in the "Vent" position. Let incubate for 8 hours.
6. After 8 hours, transfer the yogurt to a glass container and chill for 4 hours in the refrigerator.
7. Add the vanilla and honey (if using) to the yogurt and mix until well combined. Cover and place the glass bowl back in the refrigerator or divide the yogurt among airtight glass jars.

Tip: If you prefer a thicker Greek-style yogurt, let the yogurt strain through cheesecloth into a large mixing bowl overnight in the refrigerator.

Nutrition

- Calories: 149
- Total fat: 8 g.
- Saturated fat: 5 g.
- Cholesterol: 25 mg.
- Sodium: 99 mg.
- Carbohydrates: 13 g.
- Fiber: 0 g.
- Protein: 8 g.

27.   Hard-Boiled Eggs

Preparation time: 2 minutes
Cooking time: 15 minutes
Servings: 2–12
Ingredients

- 1 c. water
- 2–12 eggs

Directions

1. Place the Reversible Rack in the pot in the lower position. Add the water and arrange the eggs on the rack in a single layer.
2. Assemble the Pressure Lid, making sure the pressure release valve is in the "Seal" position. Select "Pressure" and set it to Low. Set the time to 8 minutes. Select "Start/Stop" to begin.
3. While the eggs are cooking, prepare a large bowl of ice water.
4. When pressure cooking is completedd, quickly release the pressure by moving the pressure release valve to the "Vent" position. Carefully remove the lid when the unit has finished releasing pressure.
5. Using a slotted spoon, immediately transfer the eggs to the ice water bath and allow to cool for 5 minutes.

Tip: Hard-boiled eggs with hard yolks are ideal for deviled eggs, but if you prefer runny yolks, then you will want soft-boiled eggs. For soft-boiled eggs, cook on Low for 2–3 minutes, and for medium-boiled eggs, cook on Low for 5–6 minutes.

Nutrition

- Calories: 71
- Total fat: 5 g.
- Saturated fat: 2 g.
- Cholesterol: 211 mg.
- Sodium: 70 mg.
- Carbohydrates: 0 g.
- Fiber: 0 g.
- Protein: 6 g.

28.   Easy Cheesy Egg Bake

Preparation time: 5 minutes
Cooking time: 27 minutes
Servings: 4
Ingredients

- 4 eggs
- 1 c. milk
- 1 tsp. sea salt
- 1 tsp. freshly ground black pepper
- 1 c. shredded Cheddar cheese
- 1 red bell pepper, seeded and chopped
- 8 oz. ham, chopped
- 1 c. water

Directions

1. In a medium mixing bowl, whisk together the eggs, milk, salt, and black pepper. Stir in the Cheddar cheese.
2. Place the bell pepper and ham in the multi-purpose pan or an 8-inch baking pan. Pour the egg mixture over the pepper and ham. Cover the pan with aluminum foil and place it on the Reversible Rack.
3. Pour the water into the pot. Place the rack with the pan in the pot in the lower position.
4. Assemble the Pressure Lid, making sure the pressure release valve is in the "Seal" position. Select "Pressure" and set it to High. Set the time to 20 minutes. Select "Start/Stop" to begin.
5. When pressure cooking is completedd, quickly release the pressure by moving the pressure release valve to the "Vent" position. Carefully remove the lid when the unit has finished releasing pressure.
6. When cooking is completedd, remove the pan from the pot and place it on a cooling rack. Let cool for 5 minutes, then serve.

Tip: Swap the red bell pepper for other veggies like broccoli, spinach, and onions, but stay away from those that will release water, like tomatoes, zucchini, and mushrooms. Chicken and smoked sausage make good substitutes for the ham.

Nutrition

- Calories: 332
- Total fat: 21 g.
- Saturated fat: 10 g.
- Cholesterol: 280 mg.
- Sodium: 1,693 mg.
- Carbohydrates: 6 g.
- Fiber: 1 g.
- Protein: 28 g.

29.   Crispy Bacon Hash and Baked Eggs

Preparation time: 10 minutes
Cooking time: 40 minutes
Servings: 4
Ingredients

- 6 slices bacon, chopped
- 1 yellow onion, diced
- 2 russet potatoes, peeled and diced
- 1 tsp. paprika
- 1 tsp. sea salt
- 1 tsp. freshly ground black pepper
- 1 tsp. garlic salt
- 4 eggs

Directions

1. Select "Sear/Sauté" and set it to Medium-High. Select "Start/Stop" to begin. Allow the pot to preheat for 5 minutes.
2. Once hot, add the bacon to the pot. Cook, stirring occasionally, for 5 minutes, or until the bacon is crispy.
3. Add the onion and potatoes to the pot. Sprinkle with paprika, sea salt, pepper, and garlic salt.
4. Close the Crisping Lid. Select Bake/Roast, set the temperature to 350°F, and set the time to 25 minutes. Cook, stirring occasionally until the potatoes are tender and golden brown.
5. Crack the eggs onto the surface of the hash. Close the Crisping Lid. Select Bake/Roast, set the temperature to 350°F, and set the time to 10 minutes.
6. Check the eggs after 3 minutes. Continue cooking for the remaining 7 minutes, checking occasionally until your desired doneness is achieved. Serve immediately.

Nutrition

- Calories: 364
- Total fat: 24 g.
- Saturated fat: 8 g.
- Cholesterol: 240 mg.
- Sodium: 1,008 mg.
- Carbohydrates: 24 g.
- Fiber: 2 g.
- Protein: 14 g.

30.   Upside-Down Broccoli and Cheese Quiche

Preparation time: 10 minutes
Cooking time: 20 minutes
Servings: 6
Ingredients

- 8 eggs
- ½ c. milk
- 1 tsp. sea salt
- 1 tsp. freshly ground black pepper
- 1 c. shredded Cheddar cheese
- 1 tbsp. extra-virgin olive oil
- 1 yellow onion, chopped
- 2 garlic cloves, minced
- 2 c. thinly sliced broccoli florets
- 1 refrigerated pie crust, at room temperature

Directions

1. Select "Sear/Sauté" and set it to High. Select "Start/Stop" to begin. Allow the pot to preheat for 5 minutes.
2. In a large mixing bowl, whisk together the eggs, milk, salt, and pepper. Stir in the Cheddar cheese.
3. Put the oil, onion, and garlic in the preheated pot and stir occasionally for 5 minutes. Add the broccoli florets and sauté for another 5 minutes.
4. Pour the egg mixture over the vegetables and gently stir for 1 minute (this will allow the egg mixture to temper well and ensure that it cooks evenly under the crust).
5. Lay the pie crust evenly on top of the filling mixture, folding over the edges if necessary. Make a small cut in the center of the pie crust so that steam can escape during baking.
6. Close the Crisping Lid. Select Broil and set the time to 10 minutes. Select "Start/Stop" to begin.
7. When cooking is completedd, remove the pot and place it on a heat-resistant surface. Let the quiche rest for 5–10 minutes before serving.

Nutrition

- Calories: 393
- Total fat: 26 g.
- Saturated fat: 10 g.
- Cholesterol: 304 mg.
- Sodium: 773 mg.
- Carbohydrates: 26 g.
- Fiber: 2 g.
- Protein: 16 g.

31. Simple Strawberry Jam

Preparation time: 10 minutes
Cooking time: 42 minutes
Servings: 1 ½
Ingredients

- 2 lbs. strawberries, hulled and halved
- Juice of 2 lemons
- 1 ½ c. granulated sugar

Directions

1. Place the strawberries, lemon juice, and sugar in the pot. Using a silicone potato masher, mash the ingredients together to begin to release the strawberry juices.
2. Assemble the Pressure Lid, making sure the pressure release valve is in the "Seal" position. Select "Pressure" and set it to High. Set the time to 1 minute. Select "Start/Stop" to begin.
3. When pressure cooking is completedd, allow the pressure to naturally release for 10 minutes, then quickly release any remaining pressure by moving the pressure release valve to the "Vent" position. Carefully remove the lid when the pressure has finished releasing.
4. Select "Sear/Sauté" and set it to Medium-High. Select "Start/Stop" to begin. Allow the jam to reduce for 20 minutes, or until it tightens.
5. Mash the strawberries using the silicone potato masher for a textured jam, or transfer the strawberry mixture to a food processor and purée for a smooth consistency. Let the jam cool, pour it into a glass jar, and refrigerate for up to 2 weeks.

Tip: This natural jam may be a bit looser than store-bought versions because it uses all whole ingredients. If you prefer to thicken the jam, stir in flavorless gelatin after step 4.

Nutrition

- Calories: 23
- Total fat: 0 g.
- Saturated fat: 0 g.
- Cholesterol: 0 mg.
- Sodium: 0 mg.
- Carbohydrates: 6 g.
- Fiber: 0 g.
- Protein: 0 g.

32.   Apple-Cranberry Oatmeal

Preparation time: 5 minutes
Cooking time: 27 minutes
Servings: 4
Ingredients

- 2 c. gluten-free steel-cut oats
- 3 ¾ c. water
- ¼ c. apple cider vinegar
- 1 tbsp. ground cinnamon
- ½ tsp. ground nutmeg
- ½ tsp. vanilla extract
- ½ c. dried cranberries, plus more for garnish
- 2 apples, peeled, cored, and diced
- ⅛ tsp. sea salt
- Maple syrup, for topping

Directions

1. Add the oats, water, vinegar, cinnamon, nutmeg, vanilla, cranberries, apples, and salt into the pot. Assemble the Pressure Lid, making sure the pressure release valve is in the "Seal" position. Select "Pressure" and set it to High. Set the time to 11 minutes. Select "Start/Stop" to begin.
2. When pressure cooking is completedd, allow the pressure to naturally release for 10 minutes, then quickly release any remaining pressure by moving the pressure release valve to the "Vent" position. Carefully remove the lid when the pressure has finished releasing.
3. Stir the oatmeal and serve immediately. Top with maple syrup and more dried cranberries, as desired.

Tip: If you prefer old-fashioned oats, you can substitute an equal amount of them for the steel-cut oats and reduce pressure cooking time to 6 minutes. You can also add more water if you prefer thinner oatmeal.

Nutrition

- Calories: 399
- Total fat: 6 g.
- Saturated fat: 1 g.
- Cholesterol: 0 mg.
- Sodium: 76 mg.
- Carbohydrates: 71 g.
- Fiber: 12 g.
- Protein: 14 g.

CHAPTER 5:

Snacks and Appetizers

33.   Fried Pickles

Preparation time: 10 minutes
Cooking time: 10 minutes
Servings: 4
Ingredients

- 20 dill pickle slices
- ¼ c. all-purpose flour
- ⅛ tsp. baking powder
- 3 tbsps. beer or seltzer water
- ⅛ tsp. sea salt
- 2 tbsps. water, plus more if needed
- 2 tbsps. cornstarch
- 1 ½ c. panko breadcrumbs
- 1 tsp. paprika
- 1 tsp. garlic powder
- ¼ tsp. cayenne pepper
- 2 tbsps. canola oil, divided

Directions

1. Pat the pickle slices dry and place them on a dry plate in the freezer.
2. In a medium bowl, stir together the flour, baking powder, beer, salt, and water. The batter should be of the consistency of a cake batter. If it is too thick, add more water, 1 tsp. at a time.
3. Place the cornstarch in a small shallow bowl.
4. In a separate large shallow bowl, combine the breadcrumbs, paprika, garlic powder, and cayenne pepper.
5. Remove the pickles from the freezer. Dredge each one in cornstarch. Tap off any excess, then coat in the batter. Lastly, coat evenly with the breadcrumb mixture.
6. Insert the Crisper Basket and close the hood. Select "Air Crisp," set the temperature to 360°F, and set the time to 10 minutes. Select "Start/Stop" to begin preheating.
7. When the unit beeps to signify it has preheated, place the breaded pickles in the basket, stacking them if necessary, and gently brush them with 1 tbsp. oil. Close the hood and cook for 5 minutes
8. After 5 minutes, shake the basket and gently brush the pickles with the remaining 1 tbsp. of oil. Place the basket back in the unit and close the hood to resume cooking.
9. When cooking is completedd, serve immediately.

Nutrition

- Calories: 296 Total fat: 10 g.
- Saturated fat: 1 g. Cholesterol: 0 mg.
- Sodium: 768 mg. Carbohydrates: 44 g. Fiber: 3 g.
- Protein: 7 g.

34.   Charred Shishito Peppers

Preparation time: 5 minutes
Cooking time: 10 minutes
Servings: 4
Ingredients

- 3 c. whole shishito peppers
- 2 tbsps. vegetable oil
- Flaky sea salt, for garnish

Directions

1. Insert the Grill Grate and close the hood. Select "Grill," set the temperature to Max, and set the time to 10 minutes. Select "Start/Stop" to begin preheating.
2. While the unit is preheating, in a medium bowl, toss the peppers in the oil until evenly coated.
3. When the unit beeps to signify it has preheated, place the peppers on the Grill Grate. Gently press the peppers down to maximize grill marks. Close the hood and grill for 8–10 minutes, until they are blistered on all sides.
4. When cooking is completedd, place the peppers in a serving dish and top with the flaky sea salt. Serve immediately.

Nutrition

- Calories: 83
- Total fat: 7 g.
- Saturated fat: 1 g.
- Cholesterol: 0 mg.
- Sodium: 49 mg.
- Carbohydrates: 5 g.
- Fiber: 3 g.
- Protein: 2 g.

35. Lemon-Garlic Artichokes

Preparation time: 10 minutes
Cooking time: 10 minutes
Servings: 4
Ingredients

- Juice of ½ lemon
- ½ c. canola oil
- 3 garlic cloves, chopped
- Sea salt
- Freshly ground black pepper
- 2 large artichokes, trimmed and halved

Directions

1. Insert the Grill Grate and close the hood. Select "Grill," set the temperature to Max, and set the time to 10 minutes. Select "Start/Stop" to begin preheating.
2. While the unit is preheating, in a medium bowl, combine the lemon juice, oil, and garlic. Season with salt and pepper, then brush the artichoke halves with the lemon-garlic mixture.
3. When the unit beeps to signify it has preheated, place the artichokes on the Grill Grate, cut side down. Gently press them down to maximize grill marks. Close the hood and grill for 8–10 minutes, occasionally basting generously with the lemon-garlic mixture throughout cooking, until blistered on all sides.

Nutrition

- Calories: 285
- Total fat: 28 g.
- Saturated fat: 2 g.
- Cholesterol: 0 mg.
- Sodium: 137 mg.
- Carbohydrates: 10 g.
- Fiber: 5 g.
- Protein: 3 g.

36.   Blistered Green Beans

Preparation time: 5 minutes
Cooking time: 10 minutes
Servings: 4
Ingredients

- 1 lb. haricots verts or green beans, trimmed
- 2 tbsps. vegetable oil
- Juice of 1 lemon
- 1 pinch red pepper flakes
- Flaky sea salt
- Freshly ground black pepper

Directions

1. Insert the Grill Grate and close the hood. Select "Grill," set the temperature to Max, and set the time to 10 minutes. Select "Start/Stop" to begin preheating.
2. While the unit is preheating, in a medium bowl, toss the green beans in oil until evenly coated.
3. When the unit beeps to signify it has preheated, place the green beans on the Grill Grate. Close the hood and grill for 8–10 minutes, tossing frequently until blistered on all sides.
4. When cooking is completedd, place the green beans on a large serving platter. Squeeze lemon juice over the green beans, top with red pepper flakes, and season with sea salt and black pepper.

Nutrition

- Calories: 100
- Total fat: 7 g.
- Saturated fat: 1 g.
- Cholesterol: 0 mg.
- Sodium: 30 mg.
- Carbohydrates: 10 g.
- Fiber: 4 g.
- Protein: 2 g.

37.   Bacon Brussels Sprout

Preparation time: 10 minutes

Cooking time: 12 minutes
Servings: 4
Ingredients

- 1 lb. Brussels sprouts, trimmed and halved
- 2 tbsps. extra-virgin olive oil
- 1 tsp. sea salt
- ½ tsp. freshly ground black pepper
- 6 slices bacon, chopped

Directions

1. Insert the Crisper Basket and close the hood. Select "Air Crisp," set the temperature to 390°F, and set the time to 12 minutes. Select "Start/Stop" to begin preheating.
2. Meanwhile, in a large bowl, toss the Brussels sprouts with olive oil, salt, pepper, and bacon.
3. When the unit beeps to signify it has preheated, add the Brussels sprouts to the basket. Close the hood and cook for 10 minutes.
4. After 6 minutes, shake the basket of Brussels sprouts. Place the basket back in the unit and close the hood to resume cooking.
5. After 6 minutes, check for desired crispness. Continue cooking up to 2 more minutes, if necessary.

Nutrition

- Calories: 264
- Total fat: 19 g.
- Saturated fat: 5 g.
- Cholesterol: 31 mg.
- Sodium: 1,155 mg.
- Carbohydrates: 11 g.
- Fiber: 4 g.
- Protein: 15 g.

38. Grilled Asian-Style Broccoli

Preparation time: 5 minutes
Cooking time: 10 minutes
Servings: 4
Ingredients

- 4 tbsps. soy sauce
- 4 tbsps. balsamic vinegar
- 2 tbsps. canola oil
- 2 tsps. maple syrup
- 2 heads broccoli, trimmed into florets
- Red pepper flakes, for garnish
- Sesame seeds, for garnish

Directions

1. Insert the Grill Grate and close the hood. Select "Grill," set the temperature to Max, and set the time to 10 minutes. Select "Start/Stop" to begin preheating.
2. While the unit is preheating, in a large bowl, whisk together the soy sauce, balsamic vinegar, oil, and maple syrup. Add the broccoli and toss to coat evenly.
3. When the unit beeps to signify it has preheated, place the broccoli on the Grill Grate. Close the hood and grill for 8–10 minutes, until charred on all sides.
4. When cooking is completedd, place the broccoli on a large serving platter. Garnish with red pepper flakes and sesame seeds. Serve immediately.

Nutrition

- Calories: 133
- Total fat: 8 g.
- Saturated fat: 1 g.
- Cholesterol: 0 mg.
- Sodium: 948 mg.
- Carbohydrates: 13 g.
- Fiber: 4 g.
- Protein: 5 g.

39.   Honey-Glazed Grilled Carrots

Preparation time: 10 minutes
Cooking time: 10 minutes
Servings: 4
Ingredients

- 6 medium carrots, peeled and cut lengthwise
- 1 tbsp. canola oil
- 2 tbsps. unsalted butter, melted
- ¼ c. brown sugar, melted
- ¼ c. honey
- ⅛ tsp. sea salt

Directions

1. Insert the Grill Grate and close the hood. Select "Grill," set the temperature to Max, and set the time to 10 minutes. Select "Start/Stop" to begin preheating.
2. In a large bowl, toss the carrots and oil until well coated.
3. When the unit beeps to signify it has preheated, place carrots on the center of the Grill Grate. Close the hood and cook for 5 minutes.
4. Meanwhile, in a small bowl, whisk together the butter, brown sugar, honey, and salt.
5. After 5 minutes, open the hood and baste the carrots with the glaze. Using tongs, turn the carrots and baste the other side. Close the hood and cook for another 5 minutes.
6. When cooking is completedd, serve immediately.

Nutrition

- Calories: 218
- Total fat: 9 g.
- Saturated fat: 4 g.
- Cholesterol: 15 mg.
- Sodium: 119 mg.
- Carbohydrates: 35 g.
- Fiber: 2 g.
- Protein: 1 g.

40.   Garlicky Summer Squash and Charred Red Onion

Preparation time: 15 minutes
Cooking time: 15 minutes
Servings: 4

Ingredients

- ½ c. vegetable oil, plus 3 tbsps.
- ¼ c. white wine vinegar
- 1 garlic clove, grated
- 2 summer squash, sliced lengthwise about ¼-inch thick
- 1 red onion, peeled and cut into wedges
- Sea salt
- Freshly ground black pepper
- 1 (8 oz.) package crumbled Feta cheese
- Red pepper flakes

Directions

1. Insert the Grill Grate and close the hood. Select "Grill," set the temperature to Max, and set the time to 15 minutes. Select "Start/Stop" to begin preheating.
2. Meanwhile, in a small bowl, whisk together ½ c. oil, vinegar, and garlic, and set aside.
3. In a large bowl, toss the squash and onion with the remaining 3 tbsps. of oil until evenly coated. Season with salt and pepper.
4. When the unit beeps to signify it has preheated, arrange the squash and onions on the Grill Grate. Close the hood and cook for 6 minutes.
5. After 6 minutes, open the hood and flip the squash. Close the hood and cook for 6–9 minutes more.
6. When vegetables are cooked to desired doneness, remove them from the grill. Arrange the vegetables on a large platter and top with the Feta cheese. Drizzle the dressing over the top, and sprinkle with the red pepper flakes. Let stand for 15 minutes before serving.

Nutrition

- Calories: 521
- Total fat: 50 g.
- Saturated fat: 16 g.
- Cholesterol: 50 mg.
- Sodium: 696 mg.
- Carbohydrates: 11 g.
- Fiber: 2 g.
- Protein: 10 g.

41. Crispy   Rosemary Potatoes

Preparation time: 10 minutes
Cooking time: 20 minutes
Servings: 4
Ingredients

- 2 lbs. baby red potatoes, quartered
- 2 tbsps. extra-virgin olive oil
- ¼ c. dried onion flakes
- 1 tsp. dried rosemary
- ½ tsp. onion powder
- ½ tsp. garlic powder
- ¼ tsp. celery
- ¼ tsp. freshly ground black pepper
- ½ tsp. dried parsley
- ½ tsp. sea salt

Directions

1. Insert the Crisper Basket and close the hood. Select "Air Crisp," set the temperature to 390°F, and set the time to 20 minutes. Select "Start/Stop" to begin preheating.
2. Meanwhile, place all the ingredients in a large bowl and toss until evenly coated.
3. When the unit beeps to signify it has preheated, add the potatoes to the basket. Close the hood and cook for 10 minutes.
4. After 10 minutes, shake the basket well. Place the basket back in the unit and close the hood to resume cooking.
5. After 10 minutes, check for desired crispness. Continue cooking up to 5 minutes more, if necessary.

Nutrition

- Calories: 232
- Total fat: 7 g.
- Saturated fat: 1 g.
- Cholesterol: 0 mg.
- Sodium: 249 mg.
- Carbohydrates: 39 g.
- Fiber: 6 g.
- Protein: 4 g.

42. Watermelon Jerky

Preparation time: 5 minutes
Cooking time: 12 hours
Servings: ½

Ingredients

- 1 c. seedless watermelon (1-inch) cubes

Directions

1. Arrange the watermelon cubes in a single layer in the Cook & Crisp Basket. Place the basket in the pot and close the Crisping Lid.
2. Press "Dehydrate," set the temperature to 135°F, and set the time to 12 hours. Select "Start/Stop" to begin.
3. When dehydrating is completedd, remove the basket from the pot and transfer the jerky to an airtight container.

Nutrition

- Calories: 46
- Total fat: 0 g.
- Saturated fat: 0 g.
- Cholesterol: 0 mg.
- Sodium: 6 mg.
- Carbohydrates: 12 g.
- Fiber: 1 g.
- Protein: 1 g.

43.   Dried Mango

Preparation time: 5 minutes
Cooking time: 8 hours
Servings: 2
Ingredients

- ½ mango, peeled, pitted, and cut into ⅜-inch slices

Directions

1. Arrange the mango slices flat in a single layer in the Cook & Crisp Basket. Place in the pot and close the Crisping Lid.
2. Press "Dehydrate," set the temperature to 135°F, and set the time to 8 hours. Select "Start/Stop" to begin.
3. When dehydrating is completedd, remove the basket from the pot and transfer the mango slices to an airtight container.

Nutrition

- Calories: 67
- Total fat: 0 g.
- Saturated fat: 0 g.
- Cholesterol: 0 mg.
- Sodium: 2 mg.
- Carbohydrates: 18 g.
- Fiber: 2 g.
- Protein: 1 g.

44.   Beet Chips

Preparation time: 5 minutes
Cooking time: 8 hours
Servings: ½
Ingredients

- ½ beet, peeled and cut into ⅛-inch slices

Directions

1. Arrange the beet slices flat in a single layer in the Cook & Crisp Basket. Place in the pot and close the Crisping Lid.
2. Press "Dehydrate," set the temperature to 135°F, and set the time to 8 hours. Select "Start/Stop" to begin.
3. When dehydrating is completedd, remove the basket from the pot and transfer the beet chips to an airtight container.

Nutrition

- Calories: 35
- Total fat: 0 g.
- Saturated fat: 0 g.
- Cholesterol: 0 mg.
- Sodium: 64 mg.
- Carbohydrates: 8 g.
- Fiber: 2 g.
- Protein: 1 g.

45.   Maple Candied Bacon

Preparation time: 5 minutes
Cooking time: 40 minutes
Servings: 12
Ingredients

- ½ c. maple syrup
- ¼ c. brown sugar
- Nonstick cooking spray
- 1 lb. (12 slices) thick-cut bacon

Directions

1. Place the Reversible Rack in the pot. Close the Crisping Lid. Preheat the unit by selecting "Air Crisp," setting the temperature to 400°F, and setting the time to 5 minutes.
2. Meanwhile, in a small mixing bowl, mix the maple syrup and brown sugar.
3. Once it has preheated, carefully line the Reversible Rack with aluminum foil. Spray the foil with cooking spray.
4. Arrange 4–6 slices of bacon on the rack in a single layer. Brush them with the maple syrup mixture.
5. Close the Crisping Lid. Select "Air Crisp" and set the temperature to 400°F. Set the time to 10 minutes, then Select "Start/Stop" to begin.
6. After 10 minutes, flip the bacon and brush with more maple syrup mixture. Close the Crisping Lid, Select "Air Crisp," set the temperature to 400°F, and set the time to 10 minutes. Select "Start/Stop" to begin.
7. Cooking is completedd when your desired crispiness is reached. Remove the bacon from the Reversible Rack and transfer to a cooling rack for 10 minutes. Repeat steps 4 through 6 with the remaining bacon.

Nutrition

- Calories: 451
- Total fat: 34 g.
- Saturated fat: 11 g.
- Cholesterol: 51 mg.
- Sodium: 634 mg.
- Carbohydrates: 27 g.
- Fiber: 0 g.
- Protein: 9 g.

46.   Chili-Ranch Chicken Wings

Preparation time: 10 minutes
Cooking time: 28 minutes
Servings: 4
Ingredients

- ½ c. water
- ½ c. hot pepper sauce
- 2 tbsps. unsalted butter, melted
- 1½ tbsps. apple cider vinegar
- 2 lbs. frozen chicken wings
- ½ (1 oz.) envelope ranch salad dressing mix
- ½ tsp. paprika
- Nonstick cooking spray

Directions

1. Pour the water, hot pepper sauce, butter, and vinegar into the pot. Place the wings in the Cook & Crisp Basket and place the basket in the pot. Assemble the Pressure Lid, making sure the pressure release valve is in the "Seal" position.
2. Select "Pressure" and set it to High. Set the time to 5 minutes. Select "Start/Stop" to begin.
3. When pressure cooking is completed, quickly release the pressure by turning the pressure release valve to the "Vent" position. Carefully remove the lid when the unit has finished releasing pressure.
4. Sprinkle the chicken wings with the dressing mix and paprika. Coat with cooking spray.
5. Close the Crisping Lid. Select "Air Crisp," set the temperature to 375°F, and set the time to 15 minutes. Select "Start/Stop" to begin.
6. After 7 minutes, open the Crisping Lid, then lift the basket and shake the wings. Coat with cooking spray. Lower the basket back into the pot and close the lid to resume cooking until the wings reach your desired crispiness.

Nutrition

- Calories: 405
- Total fat: 30 g.
- Saturated fat: 10 g.
- Cholesterol: 131 mg.
- Sodium: 1,782 mg.
- Carbohydrates: 4 g.
- Fiber: 0 g.
- Protein: 28 g.

47.   Crispy Cheesy Arancini

Preparation time: 15 minutes
Cooking time: 45 minutes
Servings: 6
Ingredients

- ½ c. extra-virgin olive oil, plus 1 tbsp.
- 1 small yellow onion, diced
- 2 garlic cloves, minced
- 5 c. chicken broth
- ½ c. white wine
- 2 c. arborio rice
- 1½ c. grated Parmesan cheese, plus more for garnish
- 1 c. frozen peas - 1 tsp. sea salt
- 1 tsp. freshly ground black pepper
- 2 c. fresh breadcrumbs - 2 large eggs

Directions

1. Select "Sear/Sauté" and set it to Medium-High. Select "Start/Stop" to begin. Allow the pot to preheat for 5 minutes.
2. Add 1 tbsp. of oil and the onion to the preheated pot. Cook until soft and translucent, stirring occasionally. Add the garlic and cook for 1 minute.
3. Add the broth, wine, and rice to the pot; stir to incorporate. Assemble the Pressure Lid, making sure the pressure release valve is in the "Seal" position.
4. Select "Pressure" and set it to High. Set the time to 7 minutes. Press "Start/Stop" to begin.
5. When pressure cooking is completed, allow pressure to naturally release for 10 minutes, then quickly release any remaining pressure by turning the pressure release valve to the "Vent" position. Carefully remove the lid when the unit has finished releasing pressure.
6. Add the Parmesan cheese, frozen peas, salt, and pepper. Stir vigorously until the rice begins to thicken. Transfer the risotto to a large mixing bowl and let cool.
7. Meanwhile, clean the pot. In a medium mixing bowl, stir together the breadcrumbs and the remaining ½ c. olive oil. In a separate mixing bowl, lightly beat the eggs.
8. Divide the risotto into 12 equal portions and form each one into a ball. Dip each risotto ball in the beaten eggs, then coat in the breadcrumb mixture.
9. Arrange half of the arancini in the Cook & Crisp Basket in a single layer.
10. Close the Crisping Lid. Select "Air Crisp," set the temperature to 400°F, and set the time to 10 minutes. Select "Start/Stop" to begin.
11. Repeat steps 9 and 10 to cook the remaining arancini.

Nutrition

- Calories: 769 Total fat: 32 g. Saturated fat: 9 g.
- Cholesterol: 98 mg. Sodium: 1,348 mg. Carbohydrates: 91 g.
- Fiber: 5 g. Protein: 27 g.

48.   Buffalo Chicken Meatballs

Preparation time: 10 minutes
Cooking time: 40 minutes
Servings: 6
Ingredients

- 1 lb. ground chicken
- 1 carrot, minced
- 2 celery stalks, minced
- ¼ c. crumbled blue cheese
- ¼ c. buffalo sauce
- ¼ c. breadcrumbs
- 1 egg
- 2 tbsps. extra-virgin olive oil
- ½ c. water

Directions

1. Select "Sear/Sauté" and set it to High. Select "Start/Stop" to begin. Allow the pot to preheat for 5 minutes.
2. Meanwhile, in a large mixing bowl, mix together the chicken, carrot, celery, blue cheese, buffalo sauce, breadcrumbs, and egg. Shape the mixture into 1 ½-inch meatballs.
3. Pour the olive oil into the preheated pot. Working in batches, place the meatballs in the pot and sear on all sides until browned. When each batch finishes cooking, transfer to a plate.
4. Place the Cook & Crisp Basket in the pot. Add the water, then place all the meatballs in the basket.
5. Assemble the Pressure Lid, making sure the pressure release valve is in the "Seal" position. Select "Pressure" and set it to High. Set the time to 5 minutes. Select "Start/Stop" to begin.
6. When pressure cooking is completed, quickly release the pressure by turning the pressure release valve to the "Vent" position. Carefully remove the lid when the unit has finished releasing pressure.
7. Close the Crisping Lid. Select "Air Crisp," set the temperature to 360°F, and set the time to 10 minutes. Select "Start/Stop" to begin.
8. After 5 minutes, open the lid, then lift the basket and shake the meatballs. Lower the basket back into the pot and close the lid to resume cooking until the meatballs achieve your desired crispiness.

Nutrition

- Calories: 204 Total fat: 13 g.
- Saturated fat: 4 g. Cholesterol: 104 mg.
- Sodium: 566 mg. Carbohydrates: 5 g.
- Fiber: 1 g. Protein: 16 g.

49.   Loaded Smashed Potatoes

Preparation time: 10 minutes
Cooking time: 30 minutes
Servings: 4
Ingredients

- 12 oz. baby Yukon Gold potatoes
- 1 tsp. extra-virgin olive oil
- ¼ c. sour cream
- ¼ c. shredded Cheddar cheese
- 2 slices bacon, cooked and crumbled
- 1 tbsp. chopped fresh chives
- Sea salt

Directions

1. Place the Cook & Crisp Basket in the pot. Close the Crisping Lid. Preheat the unit by selecting "Air Crisp," setting the temperature to 350°F, and setting the time to 5 minutes. Press "Start/Stop" to begin.
2. Meanwhile, toss the potatoes with the oil until evenly coated.
3. Once the pot and basket are preheated, open the lid and add the potatoes to the basket. Close the lid, Select "Air Crisp," set the temperature to 350°F, and set the time to 30 minutes. Press "Start/Stop" to begin.
4. After 15 minutes, open the lid, then lift the basket and shake the potatoes. Lower the basket back into the pot and close the lid to resume cooking.
5. After 15 minutes, check the potatoes for your desired crispiness. They should be fork-tender.
6. Remove the potatoes from the basket. Use a large spoon to lightly crush the potatoes to split them. Top with sour cream, cheese, bacon, and chives, and season with salt.

Nutrition

- Calories: 154
- Total fat: 8 g.
- Saturated fat: 4 g.
- Cholesterol: 19 mg.
- Sodium: 152 mg.
- Carbohydrates: 16 g.
- Fiber: 1 g.
- Protein: 5 g.

CHAPTER 6:

Meat Recipe

50.   Pork With Potatoes and Green Beans

Preparation time: 10 minutes
Cooking time: 15 minutes
Servings: 2
Ingredients

- ¼ c. Dijon mustard
- 2 tbsp. brown sugar
- 1 tsp. dried parsley flake
- ½ tsp. dried thyme
- ¼ tsp. salt
- ¼ tsp. ground black pepper
- 1 ¼ lbs. pork tenderloin
- ¾ lb. small potatoes, halved
- 1 (12 oz) package green beans, trimmed
- 1 tbsp. olive oil
- Salt and black pepper ground to taste

Directions

1. Preheat your Air Fryer machine to 400°F.
2. Add mustard, parsley, brown sugar, salt, black pepper, and thyme in a large bowl, then mix well.
3. Add tenderloin to the spice mixture and coat well.
4. Toss potatoes with olive oil, salt, black pepper, and green beans in another bowl.
5. Place the prepared tenderloin in Zone 1 basket.
6. Return this Air Fryer basket to the Air Fryer.
7. Select the "Air Fryer" mode for Zone 1 with 390°F temperature and 15 minutes cooking time.
8. Add potatoes and green beans to the 2nd basket.
9. Select the "Air Fryer" mode for Zone 2 with 350°F temperature and 10 minutes cooking time.
10. Press the "Smart Finish" button to sync the settings with Zone 2.
11. Start cooking by pressing the "Start/Pause" button.
12. Serve the tenderloin with the air-fried potatoes.

Nutrition

- Calories: 380 Total fat: 20 g.
- Saturated fat: 5 g. Cholesterol: 151 mg.
- Sodium: 686 mg. Total carbohydrates: 33 g.
- Fiber: 1 g. Sugar: 1.2 g.
- Protein: 21 g.

51.Mini Meatloaves

Preparation time: 10 minutes
Cooking time: 22 minutes
Servings: 4
Ingredients

- ⅓ c. milk
- 2 tbsp. basil pesto
- 1 egg, beaten
- 1 garlic clove, minced
- ¼ tsp. ground black pepper
- 1 lb. ground beef
- ⅓ c. panko breadcrumbs
- 8 pepperoni slices
- ½ c. marinara sauce, warmed
- 1 tbsp. chopped fresh basil, or to taste

Directions

1. Mix pesto, milk, egg, garlic, and black pepper in a medium-sized bowl.
2. Stir in ground beef and breadcrumbs then mix.
3. Make the 4 small-sized loaves with this mixture and top them with 2 pepperoni slices.
4. Press the slices into the meatloaves.
5. Place the meatloaves in the 2 Air Fryer baskets.
6. Return the Air Fryer baskets to the Air Fryer.
7. Select the "Air Fryer" mode for Zone 1 with 390°F temperature and 22 minutes cooking time.
8. Press the "Match Cook" button to copy the settings for Zone 2.
9. Start cooking by pressing the "Start/Pause" button.
10. Top them with marinara sauce and basil to serve.
11. Serve warm.

Nutrition

- Calories: 361
- Total fat: 16.3 g.
- Saturated fat: 4.9 g.
- Cholesterol: 114 mg.
- Sodium: 515 mg.
- Total carbohydrates: 19.3 g.
- Fiber: 0.1 g.
- Sugar: 18.2 g.
- Protein: 33.3 g.

52.   Pork Chops With Brussels Sprouts

Preparation time: 10 minutes
Cooking time: 15 minutes
Servings: 4
Ingredients

- 4 bone-in center-cut pork chop
- Cooking spray
- Salt, to taste
- Black pepper, to taste
- 2 tsp. olive oil
- 2 tsp. pure maple syrup
- 2 tsp. Dijon mustard
- 6 oz Brussels sprouts, quartered

Directions

1. Rub pork chop with salt, ¼ tsp. black pepper, and cooking spray.
2. Toss Brussels sprouts with mustard, syrup, oil, ¼ tsp. black pepper in a medium bowl.
3. Add pork chop to the Zone 1 basket of the Air Fryer.
4. Return the Air Fryer basket to the Air Fryer.
5. Select the "Air Fryer" mode for Zone 1 with 400°F temperature and 15 minutes cooking time.
6. Add the Brussels sprouts to Zone 2 and return them to the unit.
7. Select the "Air Fryer" mode for Zone 2 with 350°F temperature and 13 minutes cooking time.
8. Press the "Smart Finish" button to sync the settings with Zone 2.
9. Start cooking by pressing the "Start/Pause" button.
10. Serve warm and fresh.

Nutrition

- Calories: 405
- Total fat: 22.7 g.
- Saturated fat: 6.1 g.
- Cholesterol: 4 mg.
- Sodium: 227 mg.
- Total carbohydrates: 26.1 g.
- Fiber: 1.4 g.
- Sugar: 0.9 g.
- Protein: 45.2 g.

53.   Italian Meatballs

Preparation time: 10 minutes
Cooking time: 21 minutes
Servings: 6
Ingredients

- 1 medium shallot, minced
- 2 tbsp. olive oil
- 3 garlic cloves, minced
- ¼ c. panko crumbs
- 2 tbsp. whole milk
- ⅔ lb. lean ground beef
- ⅓ lb. bulk turkey sausage
- 1 large egg, lightly beaten
- ¼ c. parsley, chopped
- 1 tbsp. fresh thyme, chopped
- 1 tbsp. fresh rosemary, chopped
- 1 tbsp. Dijon mustard
- ½ tsp. salt

Directions

1. Preheat your oven to 400°F. Place a medium non-stick pan over medium-high heat.
2. Add oil and shallot, then sauté for 2 minutes.
3. Toss in the garlic and cook for 1 minute.
4. Remove this pan from the heat.
5. Whisk panko with milk in a large bowl and leave it for 5 minutes.
6. Add cooked shallot mixture and mix well.
7. Stir in egg, parsley, turkey sausage, beef, thyme, rosemary, salt, and mustard.
8. Mix well, then divide the mixture into 1 ½-inch balls.
9. Divide these balls into the 2 Air Fryer baskets and spray them with cooking oil.
10. Return the Air Fryer baskets to the Air Fryer.
11. Select the "Air Fryer" mode for Zone 1 with 400°F temperature and 21 minutes cooking time.
12. Press the "Match Cook" button to copy the settings for Zone 2.
13. Start cooking by pressing the "Start/Pause" button.
14. Serve warm.

Nutrition

- Calories: 545 Total fat: 36.4 g.
- Saturated fat: 10.1 g. Cholesterol: 200 mg.
- Sodium: 272 mg.Total carbohydrates: 40.7 g.
- Fiber: 0.2 g.Sugar: 0.1 g. Protein: 42.5 g.

54.   Pork Chops With Broccoli Florets

Preparation time: 10 minutes
Cooking time: 13 minutes
Servings: 4
Ingredients

- 2 (5 oz.) bone-in pork chops
- 2 tbsps. avocado oil
- ½ tsp. paprika
- ½ tsp. onion powder
- ½ tsp. garlic powder
- 1 tsp. salt, divided
- 2 c. broccoli florets
- 2 garlic cloves, minced
- Hardened butter

Directions

1. Rub the pork chops with avocado oil, garlic, paprika, and spices.
2. Add pork chop to the Zone 1 basket of the Air Fryer.
3. Return the Air Fryer basket to the Air Fryer.
4. Select the "Air Fryer" mode for Zone 1 with 400°F temperature and 12 minutes cooking time.
5. Add the broccoli to Zone 2 and return it to the unit.
6. Select the "Air Fryer" mode for Zone 2 with 375°F temperature and 13 minutes cooking time.
7. Press the "Smart Finish" button to sync the settings with Zone 2.
8. Start cooking by pressing the "Start/Pause" button.
9. Flip the pork once cooked halfway through.
10. Cut the hardened butter into cubes and place it on top of the pork chops.
11. Serve warm with crispy broccoli florets.

Nutrition

- Calories: 355
- Total fat: 17.5 g.
- Saturated fat: 4.8 g.
- Cholesterol: 283 mg.
- Sodium: 355 mg.
- Total carbohydrates: 26.4 g.
- Fiber: 1.8 g.
- Sugar: 0.8 g.
- Protein: 57.4 g.

55.   Parmesan Pork Chops

Preparation time: 10 minutes
Cooking time: 15 minutes
Servings: 4
Ingredients

- 4 boneless pork chops
- 2 tbsp. extra-virgin olive oil
- ½ c. freshly grated Parmesan
- 1 tsp. salt
- 1 tsp. paprika
- 1 tsp. garlic powder
- 1 tsp. onion powder
- ½ tsp. ground black pepper

Directions

1. Pat dry the pork chops with a paper towel and rub them with olive oil.
2. Mix Parmesan with spices in a medium bowl.
3. Rub the pork chops with Parmesan mixture.
4. Place 2 seasoned pork chops in each of the 2 Air Fryer baskets.
5. Return the Air Fryer baskets to the Air Fryer.
6. Select the "Air Fryer" mode for Zone 1 with 390°F temperature and 15 minutes cooking time.
7. Press the "Match Cook" button to copy the settings for Zone 2.
8. Start cooking by pressing the "Start/Pause" button.
9. Flip the pork chops when cooked halfway through, then resume cooking.
10. Serve warm.

Nutrition

- Calories: 301
- Total fat: 8.9 g.
- Saturated fat: 4.5 g.
- Cholesterol: 57 mg.
- Sodium: 340 mg.
- Total carbohydrates: 24.7 g.
- Fiber: 1.2 g.
- Sugar: 1.3 g.
- Protein: 15.3 g.

56.   Beef Cheeseburgers

Preparation time: 10 minutes
Cooking time: 13 minutes
Servings: 4
Ingredients

- 1 lb. ground beef
- Salt to taste
- 2 garlic cloves, minced
- 1 tbsp. soy sauce
- Black pepper to taste
- 4 American cheese slices
- 4 hamburger buns
- Mayonnaise to serve
- Lettuce to serve
- Sliced tomatoes to serve
- Thinly sliced red onion to serve

Directions

1. Mix beef with soy sauce, and garlic in a large bowl.
2. Make 4 patties of 4-inch in diameter.
3. Rub them with salt and black pepper on both sides.
4. Place the 2 patties in each of the Air Fryer baskets.
5. Return the Air Fryer baskets to the Air Fryer.
6. Select the "Air Fryer" mode for Zone 1 with 390°F temperature and 13 minutes cooking time.
7. Press the "Match Cook" button to copy the settings for Zone 2.
8. Start cooking by pressing the "Start/Pause" button.
9. Flip each patty once cooked halfway through, and resume cooking.
10. Add each patty in the hamburger buns along with mayo, tomatoes, onions, cheese, and lettuce.
11. Serve.

Nutrition

- Calories: 548
- Total fat: 22.9 g.Saturated fat: 9 g.
- Cholesterol: 105 mg.
- Sodium: 350 mg.
- Total carbohydrates: 17.5 g.
- Sugar: 10.9 g.
- Fiber: 6.3 g.
- Protein: 40.1 g.

57.   Lamb Shank With Mushroom Stir Fry

Preparation time: 10 minutes
Cooking time: 35 minutes
Servings: 4
Ingredients

- 20 mushrooms, chopped
- 2 red bell pepper, chopped
- 2 red onion, chopped
- 1 c. red wine
- 4 leeks, chopped
- 2 tsp. black pepper
- 2 tsp. salt
- 3 tbsp. fresh rosemary
- 6 garlic cloves
- 4 lamb shanks
- 3 tbsp. olive oil

Directions

1. Season the lamb shanks with salt, pepper, rosemary, and 1 tsp. olive oil.
2. Set half of the shanks in each of the Air Fryer baskets.
3. Return the Air Fryer baskets to the Air Fryer.
4. Select the "Air Fryer" mode for Zone 1 with 390°F temperature and 25 minutes cooking time.
5. Press the "Match Cook" button to copy the settings for Zone 2.
6. Start cooking by pressing the "Start/Pause" button.
7. Flip the shanks halfway through, and resume cooking.
8. Meanwhile, add and heat the remaining olive oil in a skillet.
9. Add onion and garlic to sauté for 5 minutes.
10. Add in mushrooms and cook for 5 minutes.
11. Add red wine and cook until it is absorbed
12. Stir all the remaining vegetables along with black pepper and salt.
13. Cook until vegetables are al dente.
14. Serve the air fried shanks with sautéed vegetable fry.

Nutrition

- Calories: 609 Total fat: 50.5 g.
- Saturated fat: 11.7 g. Cholesterol: 58 mg.
- Sodium: 463 mg.
- Total carbohydrates: 9.9 g.
- Fiber: 1.5 g.
- Sugar: 0.3 g.
- Protein: 29.3 g.

58.   Korean Brisket

Preparation time: 10 minutes
Cooking time: 35 minutes
Servings: 4
Ingredients

- ½ tbsp. sweet paprika
- ½ tsp. toasted sesame oil
- 2 lbs. beef brisket, cut into 4 pieces
- Kosher salt to taste
- ⅛ c. Gochujang, Korean chili paste
- Ground black pepper to taste
- 1 small onion, diced
- 2 garlic cloves, minced
- 1 tsp. Asian fish sauce
- 1 ½ tbsp. peanut oil, as needed
- ½ tbsp. grated peeled fresh ginger
- ¼ tsp. red chili flakes
- ½ c. water
- 1 tbsp. sugar-free ketchup
- 1 tbsp. soy sauce

Directions

1. Thoroughly rub the beef brisket with sesame oil, paprika, chili flakes, black pepper, and salt.
2. Divide the beef into the 2 Air Fryer baskets.
3. Return the Air Fryer baskets to the Air Fryer.
4. Select the "Air Fryer" mode for Zone 1 with 390°F temperature and 35 minutes cooking time.
5. Press the "Match Cook" button to copy the settings for Zone 2.
6. Start cooking by pressing the "Start/Pause" button.
7. Flip the brisket halfway through, and resume cooking.
8. Meanwhile, heat oil in a skillet and add ginger, onion, and garlic.
9. Sauté for 5 minutes, then add all the remaining ingredients.
10. Cook the mixture for 15 minutes approximately until well thoroughly mixed.
11. Serve the brisket with this sauce on top.

Nutrition

- Calories: 537 Total fat: 19.8 g.
- Saturated fat: 1.4 g. Cholesterol: 10 mg.
- Sodium: 719 mg.Total carbohydrates: 25.1 g. Fiber: 0.9 g.
- Sugar: 1.4 g. Protein: 37.8 g.

59.   Beef Bites With Chipotle Dip

Preparation time: 10 minutes
Cooking time: 18 minutes
Servings: 4
Ingredients

- 1 lb. beef steak, cut into chunks
- 1 large egg
- Palm oil for frying
- ½ c. Parmesan cheese, grated
- ½ c. pork panko
- ½ tsp. seasoned salt
- Pepper to taste

For the chipotle ranch dip:

- ¼ c. mayonnaise
- ¼ c. sour cream
- 1 tsp. chipotle paste
- ½ tsp. ranch dressing mix
- ¼ medium lime, juiced

Directions

1. Mix all the ingredients for chipotle ranch dip in a bowl.
2. Keep it in the refrigerator for 30 minutes.
3. Mix pork panko with salt and Parmesan.
4. Beat egg in one bowl and spread the panko mixture in another flat bowl.
5. Dip the steak chunks in the egg first, then coat them with the panko mixture.
6. Spread them in the 2 Air Fryer baskets and spray them with cooking oil.
7. Return the Air Fryer baskets to the Air Fryer.
8. Select the "Air Fryer" mode for Zone 1 with 390°F temperature and 18 minutes cooking time.
9. Press the "Match Cook" button to copy the settings for Zone 2.
10. Start cooking by pressing the "Start/Pause" button.
11. Serve with chipotle ranch and salt and pepper on top. Enjoy!

Nutrition

- Calories: 452 Total fat: 4 g.
- Saturated fat: 2 g. Cholesterol: 65 mg.
- Sodium: 220 mg.
- Total carbohydrates: 23.1 g.
- Fiber: 0.3 g.
- Sugar: 1 g.
- Protein: 26 g.

60.   Vegetable Pork Skewers

Preparation time: 10 minutes
Cooking time: 23 minutes
Servings: 6
Ingredients

- 1 large zucchini, cut 1-inch pieces
- 1 lb. boneless pork belly, cut into cubes
- 1 onion yellow, diced in squares
- 1 ½ c. grape tomatoes
- 1 garlic clove, minced
- 1 lemon, juice only
- ¼ c. olive oil
- 2 tbsp. balsamic vinegar
- 1 tsp. oregano
- Olive oil spray

Directions

1. Mix together balsamic vinegar, garlic, oregano, lemon juice, and ¼ c. olive oil in a suitable bowl.
2. Then toss in the diced pork pieces and mix well to coat.
3. Leave the seasoned pork to marinate for 60 minutes in the refrigerator.
4. Take suitable wooden skewers for your Air Fryer's Basket, and then thread marinated pork and vegetables on each skewer in an alternating manner.
5. Place half of the skewers in each of the Air Fryer baskets and spray them with cooking oil.
6. Return the Air Fryer baskets to the Air Fryer.
7. Select the "Air Fryer" mode for Zone 1 with 390°F temperature and 23 minutes cooking time.
8. Press the "Match Cook" button to copy the settings for Zone 2.
9. Start cooking by pressing the "Start/Pause" button.
10. Flip the skewers once cooked halfway through, and resume cooking.
11. Serve warm.

Nutrition

- Calories: 301 Total fat: 15.8 g.
- Saturated fat: 2.7 g. Cholesterol: 75 mg.
- Sodium: 389 mg.
- Total carbohydrates: 11.7 g.
- Fiber: 0.3g
- Sugar: 0.1 g.
- Protein: 28.2 g.

61.Dijon Lamb Chops

Preparation time: 10 minutes
Cooking time: 27 minutes
Servings: 4
Ingredients

- 1 tsp. Dijon mustard
- 1 tsp. olive oil
- ½ tsp. soy sauce
- ½ tsp. garlic, minced
- ½ tsp. cumin powder
- ½ tsp. cayenne pepper
- ½ tsp. Italian spice blend
- ⅛ tsp. salt
- 4 pieces of lamb chops

Directions

1. Mix Dijon mustard, soy sauce, olive oil, garlic, cumin powder, cayenne pepper, Italian spice blend, and salt, in a medium bowl and mix well.
2. Place lamb chops into a Ziplock bag and pour in the marinade.
3. Press the air out of the bag and seal tightly.
4. Press the marinade around the lamb chops to fully coat.
5. Keep them in the fridge and marinate for at least 30 minutes, up to overnight.
6. Place 2 chops in each of the Air Fryer baskets and spray them with cooking oil.
7. Return the Air Fryer baskets to the Air Fryer.
8. Select the "Roast" mode for Zone 1 with 350°F temperature and 27 minutes cooking time.
9. Press the "Match Cook" button to copy the settings for Zone 2.
10. Start cooking by pressing the "Start/Pause" button.
11. Flip the chops once cooked halfway through, and resume cooking.
12. Switch the Air Fryer to "Air Broil" mode and cook for 5 minutes.
13. Serve warm.

Nutrition

- Calories: 308
- Total fat: 20.5 g.
- Saturated fat: 3 g.
- Cholesterol: 42 mg.
- Sodium: 688 mg.
- Total carbohydrates: 40.3 g.
- Sugar: 1.4 g.
- Fiber: 4.3 g.
- Protein: 49 g.

62.   Beef-Pepper Kabobs

Preparation time: 10 minutes
Cooking time: 20 minutes
Servings: 8
Ingredients

- 1 lb. beef chunk, stew meat, cubed
- ⅓ c. low-fat sour cream
- 2 tbsp. soy sauce
- 8 (6-inch) skewers
- 1 bell peppers, squared
- ½ onion, squared
- Salt and black pepper, to taste

Directions

1. Whisk sour cream with soy sauce in a medium bowl then toss in beef chunks.
2. Mix well then cover to refrigerate for 30 minutes.
3. Thread the beef, onion, and bell peppers over the skewers alternately.
4. Drizzle the salt and black pepper over the skewers.
5. Place half of the skewers in each of the Air Fryer baskets and spray them with cooking oil.
6. Return the Air Fryer baskets to the Air Fryer.
7. Select the "Roast" mode for Zone 1 with 390°F temperature and 20 minutes cooking time.
8. Press the "Match Cook" button to copy the settings for Zone 2.
9. Start cooking by pressing the "Start/Pause" button.
10. Flip the skewers once cooked halfway through, and resume cooking.
11. Serve warm.

Nutrition

- Calories: 231
- Total fat: 20.1 g.
- Saturated fat: 2.4 g.
- Cholesterol: 110 mg.
- Sodium: 941 mg.
- Total carbohydrates: 20.1 g.
- Fiber: 0.9 g.
- Sugar: 1.4 g.
- Protein: 34.6 g.

63.   Sriracha Steak Skewers

Preparation time: 10 minutes
Cooking time: 28 minutes
Servings: 4
Ingredients

- 1 lb. lean steak, cubed
- 2 c. mix vegetables, sliced
- ½ c. soy sauce
- ½ c. Worcestershire sauce
- ¼ c. olive oil
- ¼ c. light brown sugar
- 2 tbsps. spicy mustard
- 1 tbsp. pink Himalayan salt
- 1 tbsp. sesame oil
- 1 tsp. sriracha
- 1 tsp. red pepper flakes

Directions

1. Whisk all the ingredients, except the beef in a large bowl to prepare the marinade.
2. Toss in the beef cubes and vegetables mix well to coat.
3. Cover the saucy beef mixture and refrigerate to marinate for 2 hours approximately.
4. Start threading the veggies and beef alternately on the wooden skewers.
5. Place these veggie-beef skewers in each of the Air Fryer baskets and spray them with cooking oil.
6. Return the Air Fryer baskets to the Air Fryer.
7. Select the "Roast" mode for Zone 1 with 390°F temperature and 28 minutes cooking time.
8. Press the "Match Cook" button to copy the settings for Zone 2.
9. Start cooking by pressing the "Start/Pause" button.
10. Flip the skewers once cooked halfway through, and resume cooking.
11. Serve warm.

Nutrition

- Calories: 472
- Total fat: 11.1 g.
- Saturated fat: 5.8 g.
- Cholesterol: 610 mg.
- Sodium: 749 mg.
- Total carbohydrates: 19.9 g.
- Fiber: 0.2 g.
- Sugar: 0.2 g.
- Protein: 23.5 g.

64.   Pork Pineapple Skewers

Preparation time: 10 minutes
Cooking time: 23 minutes
Servings: 8
Ingredients

- 4 thick-cut boneless pork chops, cut into chunks
- 2 fresh pineapple, cut into chunks
- 2 tbsp. chopped fresh parsley
- 8 skewers

Directions

1. Thread the pineapple and pork chunks over the wooden skewers.
2. Divide these skewers into the 2 Air Fryer baskets and spray them with cooking oil.
3. Return the Air Fryer baskets to the Air Fryer.
4. Select the "Roast" mode for Zone 1 with 390°F temperature and 23 minutes cooking time.
5. Press the "Match Cook" button to copy the settings for Zone 2.
6. Start cooking by pressing the "Start/Pause" button.
7. Flip the skewers once cooked half through and resume cooking.
8. Serve warm.

Nutrition

- Calories: 327
- Total fat: 3.5 g.
- Saturated fat: 0.5 g.
- Cholesterol: 162 mg.
- Sodium: 142 mg.
- Total carbohydrates: 33.6 g.
- Fiber: 0.4 g.
- Sugar: 0.5 g.
- Protein: 24.5 g.

65. Pork Skewers With Mango Salsa

Preparation time: 10 minutes
Cooking time: 18 minutes
Servings: 4
Ingredients

- 2 tbsps. white sugar
- 4 ½ tsps. onion powder
- 4 ½ tsps. dried thyme, crushed
- 1 tbsp. ground allspice
- 1 tbsp. ground black pepper
- 1 ½ tsps. cayenne pepper, or to taste
- 1 ½ tsps. salt - ¾ tsp. ground nutmeg
- ¼ tsp. ground cloves - ¼ c. shredded coconut
- 1 (1 lb.) pork tenderloin, cubed
- 4 bamboo skewers, soaked, drained - 1 tbsp. vegetable oil
- 1 mango peeled, seeded, and chopped
- ½ (15 oz.) can black beans, rinsed and drained
- ¼ c. finely chopped red onion - 2 tbsps. fresh lime juice - 1 tbsp. honey
- 1 tbsp. chopped fresh cilantro
- ¼ tsp. salt - ⅛ tsp. ground black pepper

Directions

1. Start by mixing sugar, thyme, onion powder, black pepper, allspice, salt, nutmeg, cloves, and cayenne pepper in a bowl.
2. Take one 1 tbsp. of this seasoning in a bowl and preserve the rest in an airtight container.
3. Add coconut to this 1 tbsp. seasoning and mix it well.
4. Stir in the pork chunks and toss well to coat them with the seasoning.
5. Thread the pork meat over the wooden skewers.
6. Place half of these skewers in each of the Air Fryer baskets and spray them with cooking oil. Return the Air Fryer baskets to the Air Fryer.
7. Select the "Air Fryer" mode for Zone 1 with 350°F temperature and 18 minutes cooking time.
8. Press the "Match Cook" button to copy the settings for Zone 2.
9. Start cooking by pressing the "Start/Pause" button.
10. During this time, mix mango, onion, and all remaining ingredients in a salad bowl.
11. Serve the pork skewers with mango salsa. Enjoy!

Nutrition

- Calories: 353 Total fat: 7.5 g.Saturated fat: 1.1 g. Cholesterol: 20 mg. Sodium: 297 mg.
- Total carbohydrates: 10.4 g. Fiber: 0.2 g.Sugar: 0.1 g. Protein: 33.1 g.

66. Korean Chili Pork

Preparation time: 5–10 minutes
Cooking time: 8 minutes
Servings: 4
Ingredients

- 2 lbs. pork, cut into ⅛-inch slices
- 5 minced garlic cloves
- 3 tbsps. minced green onion
- 1 yellow onion, sliced
- ½ c. soy sauce
- ½ c. brown sugar
- 3 tbsps. Korean red chili paste or regular chili paste
- 2 tbsps. sesame seeds
- 3 tsps. black pepper
- Red pepper flakes to taste

Directions

1. Take a Ziplock bag and add all the ingredients. Shake well and refrigerate for 6–8 hours to marinate.
2. Take Foodi Grill, put it over your kitchen stage, and open the top.
3. Mastermind the barbecue mesh and close the top cover.
4. Click "Grill" and choose the "Med Grill" function. Flame broil work. Modify the clock to 8 minutes and press "Start/Stop." Foodi will begin to warm up.
5. Foodi is preheated and prepared to cook when it begins to signal. After you hear a signal, open the top.
6. Fix finely sliced pork on the barbeque mesh.
7. Cover and cook for 4 minutes. Then open the cover and flip the pork.
8. Cover it and cook for another 4 minutes.
9. Serve warm with chopped lettuce (optional).

Nutrition

- Calories: 621
- Fat: 31 g.
- Saturated fat: 12.5 g.
- Trans fat: 0 g.
- Carbohydrates: 29 g.
- Fiber: 3 g.
- Sodium: 1,428 mg.
- Protein: 53 g.

67.   Grilled Steak and Potatoes

Preparation time: 20 minutes
Cooking time: 50 minutes
Servings: 4
Ingredients

- 4 potatoes
- 3 sirloin steaks
- ¼ c. avocado oil
- 2 tbsps. steak seasoning
- Salt to taste

Directions

1. Poke potatoes with a fork.
2. Coat potatoes with half of the avocado oil.
3. Season with salt.
4. Add to the Air Fryer basket.
5. Choose the Air Fry function in your Foodi Grill.
6. Seal the hood and cook at 400°F for 35 minutes.
7. Flip and cook for another 10 minutes.
8. Transfer to a plate.
9. Add the Grill Grate to the Foodi Grill.
10. Add steaks to the Grill Grate.
11. Set it to High.
12. Cook for 7 minutes per side.
13. Serve steaks with potatoes.

Serving suggestions: Serve with steak sauce and hot sauce.
Preparation/cooking tips: Press steaks onto the grill to give it grill marks.
Nutrition

- Calories: 245
- Fat: 26 g.
- Carbohydrates: 7 g.
- Protein: 19 g.

68.   Roast Beef With Garlic

Preparation time: 15 minutes
Cooking time: 1 hour and 20 minutes
Servings: 4
Ingredients

- 2 lbs. beef roast, sliced
- 2 tbsps. vegetable oil
- Salt and pepper to taste
- 6 garlic cloves

Directions

1. Coat beef roast with oil.
2. Season with salt and pepper.
3. Place them inside the Foodi Grill pot.
4. Sprinkle garlic on top.
5. Choose the Bake setting.
6. Set it to 400°F and cook for 30 minutes.
7. Reduce temperature to 375°F and cook for another 40 minutes.

Serving suggestions: Serve with mashed potato and gravy.
Preparation/cooking tips: If refrigerated, let beef come to room temperature 2 hours before cooking.
Nutrition

- Calories: 390
- Fat: 29 g.
- Carbohydrates: 5 g.
- Protein: 20 g.

69.   Generous Pesto Beef Meal

Preparation time: 10 minutes
Cooking time: 14 minutes
Servings: 4
Ingredients

- ½ tsp. pepper
- ½ tsp. salt
- ½ c. Feta cheese, crumbled
- 2 /3 c. pesto
- ½ c. walnuts, chopped
- 4 c. grape tomatoes halved
- 4 c. penne pasta, uncooked
- 10 oz. baby spinach, chopped
- 4 beef (6 oz. each) tenderloin steaks

Directions

1. Cook the pasta according to the package instructions.
2. Drain the pasta and rinse it.
3. Keep the pasta on the side.
4. Season the tenderloin steaks with pepper and salt.
5. Preheat your Foodi Grill to High and set the timer to 7 minutes.
6. You will hear a beep once the preheating sequence is completed.
7. Transfer steak to your grill and cook for 7 minutes, flip and cook for 7 minutes more.
8. Take a bowl and add pasta, walnuts, spinach, tomatoes, and pesto.
9. Mix well.
10. Garnish your steak with cheese and serve with the prepared sauce.
11. Enjoy!

Nutrition

- Calories: 361
- Fat: 5 g.
- Saturated fat: 1 g.
- Carbohydrates: 16 g.
- Fiber: 4 g.
- Sodium: 269 mg.
- Protein: 33 g.

70.   Authentic Korean Flank Steak

Preparation time: 10 minutes
Cooking time: 10 minutes
Servings: 4
Ingredients

- 1 tsp. red pepper flakes
- ½ c. and 1 tbsp. soy sauce
- 1 ½ lbs. flank steak
- ¼ c. vegetable oil, plus 2 tbsps.
- ½ c. rice wine vinegar
- 3 tbsps. sriracha
- 4 garlic cloves, minced
- 2 tbsps. ginger, minced
- 2 tbsps. honey
- 3 tbsps. sesame oil
- 1 tsp. sugar
- Salt to taste

Directions

1. Take a bowl and add ½ c. soy sauce, half of the rice wine, honey, ginger, garlic, 2 tbsps. of sriracha, 2 tbsps. of sesame oil, and vegetable oil.
2. Mix well, pour half of the mixture over the steak, and rub well.
3. Cover the steak and let it sit for 10 minutes.
4. Prepare the salad mix by adding the remaining rice wine vinegar, sesame oil, sugar, red pepper flakes, sriracha sauce, soy sauce, and salt in a salad bowl.
5. Preheat your Foodi Grill on High, with the timer set to 12 minutes.
6. Transfer steak to your Grill and cook for 6 minutes per side.
7. Slice and serve with the salad mix.
8. Enjoy!

Nutrition

- Calories: 327
- Fat: 4 g.
- Saturated fat: 0.5 g.
- Carbohydrates: 33 g.
- Fiber: 1 g.
- Sodium: 142 mg.
- Protein: 24 g.

71.Garlic Butter Pork

Preparation time: 10 minutes
Cooking time: 20 minutes
Servings: 4
Ingredients

- 1 tbsp. coconut butter
- 1 tbsp. coconut oil
- 2 tsps. garlic cloves, grated
- 2 tsps. parsley
- Salt and pepper to taste
- 4 pork chops, sliced into strips

Directions

1. Combine all the ingredients, except the pork strips. Mix well.
2. Marinate the pork in the mixture for 1 hour. Put the pork on the Foodi basket.
3. Set it inside the pot. Seal with the Crisping Lid. Choose the "Air Crisp."
4. Cook at 400°F for 10 minutes.

Serving suggestion: Serve with a fresh garden salad.
Nutrition

- Calories: 388
- Total fat: 23.3 g.
- Saturated fat: 10.4 g.
- Cholesterol: 69 mg.
- Sodium: 57 mg.
- Total Carbohydrate: 0.5 g.
- Dietary fiber: 0.1 g.
- Total sugar: 0 g.
- Protein: 18.1 g.
- Potassium: 285 mg.

72.   Pork With Gravy

Preparation time: 10 minutes
Cooking time: 30 minutes
Servings: 4
Ingredients

- 5 pork chops
- 1 tbsp. olive oil
- 1 tsp. salt
- ½ tsp. pepper
- ½ tsp. garlic powder
- 2 c. beef broth
- 1 packet ranch dressing mix
- 10 ½ oz. cream of chicken soup
- 1 packet brown gravy mix
- 2 tbsps. cornstarch dissolved in 2 tbsps. water

Directions

1. Season both sides of the pork chops with salt, pepper, and garlic powder.
2. Pour the olive oil into the Foodi. Set it to Sauté.
3. Brown the pork chops on both sides. Remove and set aside.
4. Pour the beef broth to deglaze the pot.
5. Add the rest of the ingredients, except the cornstarch. Seal the pot.
6. Set it to "Pressure." Cook at high pressure for 8 minutes. Release the pressure naturally.
7. Remove the pork chops. Turn the pot to Sauté. Stir in the cornstarch.
8. Simmer to thicken. Pour the gravy over the pork chops.

Nutrition

- Calories: 357
- Total fat: 26.8 g.
- Saturated fat: 9 g.
- Cholesterol: 74 mg.
- Sodium: 1,308 mg.
- Total Carbohydrate: 6 g.
- Dietary fiber: 0.1 g.
- Total sugar: 0.8 g.
- Protein: 21.6 g.
- Potassium: 396 mg.

73.   Hawaiian Pork

Preparation time: 10 minutes
Cooking time: 20 minutes
Servings: 4
Ingredients

- 20 oz. pineapple chunks, undrained
- 2 tbsps. soy sauce
- 3 tbsps. honey
- 1 tbsp. ginger, grated
- 2 tbsps. brown sugar
- 3 garlic cloves, minced
- 2 tbsps. olive oil, divided
- 1 onion, chopped
- 2 lbs. pork stew meat
- 1 tsp. oregano

Directions

1. Mix the pineapple juice, soy sauce, honey, ginger, sugar, and garlic in a bowl. Set aside. Set the Foodi to Sauté. Add half of the oil. Cook the onion for 1 minute.
2. Add the remaining oil. Brown the pork on both sides.
3. Add the pineapple chunks, oregano, and pineapple juice mixture.
4. Cover the pot. Set it to "Pressure." Cook on high pressure for 10 minutes.
5. Release the pressure naturally.

Nutrition

- Calories: 384
- Total fat: 27 g.
- Saturated fat: 9 g.
- Cholesterol: 81 mg.
- Sodium: 317 mg.
- Total carbohydrates: 13 g.
- Sugars: 10 g.
- Protein: 20 g.
- Potassium: 390 mg.

74.   Middle Eastern Lamb Stew

Preparation time: 10 minutes
Cooking time: 20 minutes
Servings: 4
Ingredients

- 2 tbsps. olive oil
- 1 ½ lbs. lamb stew meat, sliced into cubes
- 1 onion, diced
- 6 garlic cloves, chopped
- 1 tsp. cumin
- 1 tsp. coriander
- 1 tsp. turmeric
- 1 tsp. cinnamon
- Salt and pepper to taste
- 2 tbsps. tomato paste
- ¼ c. red wine vinegar
- 2 tbsps. honey
- 1 ¼ c. chicken broth
- 15 oz. chickpeas, rinsed and drained
- ¼ c. raisins

Directions

1. Choose Sauté on the Foodi. Add the oil. Cook the onion for 3 minutes.
2. Add the lamb and seasonings. Cook for 5 minutes, stirring frequently.
3. Stir in the rest of the ingredients. Cover the pot. Set it to "Pressure."
4. Cook on high pressure for 50 minutes. Release the pressure naturally.

Nutrition

- Calories: 867
- Total fat: 26.6 g.
- Saturated fat: 6.3 g.
- Cholesterol: 153 mg.
- Sodium: 406 mg.
- Total Carbohydrate: 87.4 g.
- Dietary fiber: 20.4 g.
- Total sugar: 27.9 g.
- Protein: 71.2 g.
- Potassium: 1,815 mg.

75.   Lamb Curry

Preparation time: 10 minutes
Cooking time: 10 minutes
Servings: 4
Ingredients

- 1 ½ lbs. lamb stew meat, cubed
- 1 tbsp. lime juice
- 4 garlic cloves, minced
- ½ c. coconut milk
- 1-inch piece fresh ginger, grated
- Salt and pepper to taste
- 1 tbsp. coconut oil
- 14 oz. diced tomatoes
- ¾ tsp. turmeric
- 1 tbsp. curry powder
- 1 onion, diced
- 3 carrots, sliced

Directions

1. In a bowl, toss the lamb meat in lime juice, garlic, coconut milk, ginger, salt, and pepper. Marinate for 30 minutes.
2. Put the meat with its marinade and the rest of the ingredients into the Foodi.
3. Mix well. Seal the pot. Set it to "Pressure." Cook at high pressure for 20 minutes.
4. Release the pressure naturally.

Nutrition

- Calories: 631
- Total fat: 31.4 g.
- Saturated fat: 18.4 g.
- Cholesterol: 204 mg.
- Sodium: 230 mg.
- Total Carbohydrate: 19.7 g.
- Dietary fiber: 5.7 g.
- Total sugar: 9.5 g.
- Protein: 67.2 g.
- Potassium: 1,490 mg.

76.   Asparagus Tomato Beef

Preparation time: 35–40 minutes
Cooking time: 70 minutes
Servings: 4
Ingredients

- ½ lb. asparagus, trimmed, steamed and halved
- 1 c. tomato puree
- 1 lb. beef stew meat, cut into cubes
- 2 tbsps. ginger, grated
- 1 pinch of black pepper (finely ground) and salt
- 1 yellow onion, chopped
- 1 tbsp. olive oil

Directions

1. Take your Foodi and place it over a dry kitchen platform. Plug it in and open the lid.
2. Pour the oil into the pot. Press the "Sear/Sauté" cooking function. Adjust temperature level to Medium-High.
3. Press the "Start/Stop" button to start the cooking process. It will take 3–5 minutes to preheat.
4. When the oil is simmering, add the meat and brown for 4–5 minutes.
5. Add the onion, ginger, black pepper, and salt; stir and cook for 4 minutes more.
6. Mix in the tomato puree; stir the mixture using a spatula.
7. Close the top by placing the pressing lid. Do not forget to set the temperature valve in a "Seal" position.
8. Press the "Pressure" cooking function. Adjust and set pressure level to High.
9. Adjust cooking time to 15 minutes. Press the "Start/Stop" button to start the cooking process.
10. After cooking time is over, allow the build-up pressure to get released for around 10 minutes in a natural manner. Then, set the pressure valve to the "Vent" position in order to release the remaining pressure quicker.
11. Open the lid; mix in the asparagus.
12. Press the "Sear/Sauté" cooking function. Adjust temperature level to Medium-High. Stir and cook for 4–5 minutes.
13. Divide into serving plates or bowls; serve warm.

Nutrition

- Calories: 273 Fat: 11 g.
- Carbohydrates 8 g. Fiber: 2 g.
- Protein: 36 g.

77.   Green Bean Pork Dinner

Preparation time: 25 minutes
Cooking time: 30 minutes
Servings: 4
Ingredients

- 2 garlic cloves, minced
- 1 tbsp. basil, chopped
- 2 lbs. pork stew meat, cut into cubes
- 1 tbsp. avocado oil
- 1 lb. green beans, trimmed and halved
- 1 tsp. chili powder
- ¾ c. veggie stock
- 1 pinch of black pepper (finely ground) and salt

Directions

1. Take your Foodi and place it over a dry kitchen platform. Plug it in and open the lid.
2. Pour the oil into the pot. Press the "Sear/Sauté" cooking function. Adjust temperature level to Medium-High.
3. Press the "Start/Stop" button to start the cooking process. It will take 3–5 minutes to preheat.
4. When the oil is simmering, add the meat and garlic, stir and cook to evenly brown for 3–4 minutes.
5. Add the remaining ingredients; stir the mixture using a spatula.
6. Close the top by placing the pressing lid. Do not forget to set the temperature valve in a "Seal" position.
7. Press the "Pressure" cooking function. Adjust and set pressure level to High.
8. Adjust cooking time to 20 minutes. Press the "Start/Stop" button to start the cooking process.
9. After cooking time is over, allow the build-up pressure to get released for around 10 minutes in a natural manner. Then, set the pressure valve to the "Vent" position in order to release the remaining pressure quicker.
10. Divide into serving plates or bowls; serve warm.

Nutrition

- Calories: 429
- Fat: 16 g.
- Carbohydrates 14 g.
- Fiber: 4 g.
- Protein: 58 g.

78.   Chorizo Cashew Soup

Preparation time: 15 minutes
Cooking time: 20 minutes
Servings: 5–6
Ingredients

- 2 shallots, sliced
- 3 garlic cloves, minced
- 3 chorizo sausage, chopped
- 28 oz. fire-roasted diced tomatoes
- ½ c. ripe tomatoes
- 1 tbsp. red wine vinegar
- ½ c. thinly sliced fresh basil
- 4 c. beef broth
- ½ c. raw cashews
- 1 tbsp. olive oil
- 1 tsp. salt
- ½ tsp. ground black pepper

Directions

1. Take your Foodi and place it over a dry kitchen platform. Plug it in and open the lid.
2. Pour the oil into the pot. Press the "Sear/Sauté" cooking function. Adjust temperature level to Medium-High.
3. Press the "Start/Stop" button to start the cooking process. It will take 3–5 minutes to preheat.
4. When the oil is simmering, add the chorizo, stir, and cook until crisp. Remove and transfer to a plate lined with a paper towel.
5. Add the garlic and shallots; stir and cook to soften and turn translucent for 4–5 minutes. Season with salt.
6. Stir in the wine vinegar, broth, diced tomatoes, cashews, tomatoes, and black pepper.
7. Close the top by placing the pressing lid. Do not forget to set the pressure valve to a "Seal" position.
8. Press the "Pressure" cooking function. Adjust temperature level to High.
9. Adjust cooking time to 8 minutes. Press the "Start/Stop" button to start the cooking process.
10. After cooking time is over, set the pressure valve to the "Vent" position in order to release the build-up pressure quicker.
11. Add the mixture to a blender; blend to make a smooth soup.
12. Divide into serving plates or bowls; serve warm top with some basil and crisped chorizo.

Nutrition

- Calories: 347 Fat: 22 g. Carbohydrates 17 g. Fiber: 4 g.
- Protein: 14 g.

79. Broccoli Pork Meal

Preparation time: 35–40 minutes
Cooking time: 25 minutes
Servings: 4
Ingredients

- 2 tsps. thyme, dried
- 1 lb. broccoli florets
- 4 pork chops
- 2 tbsps. avocado oil or vegetable oil
- ½ tsp. basil, dried
- 1 c. canned tomatoes, drained and chopped
- 1 pinch of Black pepper (finely-ground) and salt
- 1 tbsp. lime juice

Directions

1. Take your Foodi and place it over a dry kitchen platform. Plug it in and open the lid.
2. Pour the oil into the pot. Press the "Sear/Sauté" cooking function. Adjust temperature level to Medium-High.
3. Press the "Start/Stop" button to start the cooking process. It will take 3–5 minutes to preheat.
4. When the oil is simmering, add the meat and brown for 5–6 minutes.
5. Add the broccoli and the rest of the ingredients. Stir the mixture.
6. Install the Reversible Rack in the pot. Place the Crisping Basket into the pot.
7. Close the top by placing the Crisping Lid. Do not forget to set the pressure valve to a "Seal" position.
8. Press the "Air Crisp" cooking function. Adjust temperature level to 390°F.
9. Adjust cooking time to 15 minutes. Press the "Start/Stop" button to start the cooking process.
10. After cooking time is over, set the pressure valve to the "Vent" position in order to release the build-up pressure quicker.
11. Divide into serving plates or bowls; serve warm.

Nutrition

- Calories: 287
- Fat: 9 g.
- Carbohydrates 13 g.
- Fiber: 4 g.
- Protein: 21 g.

80.   Bacon Potato Salad

Preparation time: 20 minutes
Cooking time: 15 minutes
Servings: 5–6
Ingredients

- 6 slices smoked bacon, chopped
- 2 red onions, sliced
- 6 red potatoes, peeled and quartered
- ½ c. water
- 1 tsp. flat-leaf parsley, chopped
- 2 tsps. mustard
- ½ c. apple cider vinegar
- 3 tbsps. honey
- 1 tsp. salt
- ⅓ tsp. black pepper

Directions

1. Take your Foodi and place it over a dry kitchen platform. Plug it in and open the lid.
2. Press the "Sear/Sauté" cooking function. Adjust temperature level to Medium-High.
3. Press the "Start/Stop" button to start the cooking process. It will take 3–5 minutes to preheat.
4. In the pot, add the bacon and cook until crispy on both sides for 3–4 minutes. Set aside.
5. In a mixing bowl (medium-large size), combine honey, salt, mustard, vinegar, water, and black pepper.
6. In the pot, combine the potatoes, chopped bacon, honey mixture, and onions; stir the mixture.
7. Close the top by placing the pressing lid. Do not forget to set the temperature valve in a "Seal" position.
8. Press the "Pressure" cooking function. Adjust and set pressure level to High.
9. Adjust cooking time to 6 minutes. Press the "Start/Stop" button to start the cooking process.
10. After cooking time is over, allow the build-up pressure to get released for around 10 minutes in a natural manner. Then, set the pressure valve to the "Vent" position in order to release the remaining pressure quicker.
11. Divide into serving plates or bowls; serve warm with some parsley on top.

Nutrition

- Calories: 413
- Fat: 17 g.
- Carbohydrates 47 g.
- Fiber: 4 g.
- Protein: 13 g.

81.Kale Beef Congee

Preparation time: 30 minutes
Cooking time: 40 minutes
Servings: 5–6
Ingredients

- 2 garlic cloves, minced
- 6 c. beef stock
- 2 lbs. ground beef
- 1 (1-inch) piece fresh ginger, minced
- 1 c. Jasmine rice, uncooked, rinsed, and drained
- 1 c. kale, roughly chopped
- 1 c. water
- Ground black pepper and salt to taste
- Fresh cilantro, chopped

Directions

1. Take your Foodi and place it over a dry kitchen platform. Plug it in and open the lid.
2. Add the garlic, rice, and ginger into the cooking pot.
3. Pour the stock and water. Stir the mixture using a spatula. Add the beef on top.
4. Close the top by placing the pressing lid. Do not forget to set the temperature valve in a "Seal" position.
5. Press the "Pressure" cooking function. Adjust and set pressure level to High.
6. Adjust cooking time to 30 minutes. Press the "Start/Stop" button to start the cooking process.
7. After cooking time is over, allow the build-up pressure to get released for around 10 minutes in a natural manner. Then, set the pressure valve to the "Vent" position in order to release the remaining pressure quicker.
8. Stir in the kale. Season with pepper and salt. Mix everything one more time.
9. Divide into serving plates or bowls; serve warm topped with some cilantro.

Nutrition

- Calories: 334
- Fat: 16 g.
- Carbohydrates 10 g.
- Fiber: 2 g.
- Protein: 36 g.

82.   Creamy Pork Sprouts

Preparation time: 35 minutes
Cooking time: 40 minutes
Servings: 4
Ingredients

- 1 lb. Brussels sprouts halved
- ½ c. heavy cream
- 4 pork chops
- 2 tbsps. avocado oil
- 1 tbsp. coconut aminos
- 1 tbsp. chives, chopped
- 1 pinch of black pepper (finely ground) and salt

Directions

1. Take your Foodi and place it over a dry kitchen platform. Plug it in and open the lid.
2. Pour the oil into the pot. Press the "Sear/Sauté" cooking function. Adjust temperature level to Medium-High.
3. Press the "Start/Stop" button to start the cooking process. It will take 3–5 minutes to preheat.
4. When the oil is simmering, add the meat and brown for 4–5 minutes.
5. Add the rest of the ingredients, except the chives. Stir the mixture using a spatula.
6. Close the top by placing the pressing lid. Do not forget to set the temperature valve in a "Seal" position.
7. Press the "Pressure" cooking function. Adjust and set pressure level to High.
8. Adjust cooking time to 20 minutes. Press the "Start/Stop" button to start the cooking process.
9. After cooking time is over, allow the build-up pressure to get released for around 10 minutes in a natural manner. Then, set the pressure valve to the "Vent" position in order to release the remaining pressure quicker.
10. Divide into serving plates or bowls; serve warm topped with some chives.

Nutrition

- Calories: 368
- Fat: 19 g.
- Carbohydrates 16 g.
- Fiber: 5 g.
- Protein: 23 g.

CHAPTER 7:

Seafood Recipes

83.   Spinach Scallops

Preparation time: 10 minutes
Cooking time: 13 minutes
Servings: 4
Ingredients

- ¾ c. heavy whipping cream
- 1 tbsp. tomato paste
- 1 tbsp. chopped fresh basil
- 1 tsp. minced garlic
- ½ tsp. salt
- ½ tsp. pepper
- 12 oz frozen spinach thawed
- 8 jumbo sea scallops
- Vegetable oil to spray

Directions

1. Season the scallops with vegetable oil, salt, and pepper in a bowl
2. Mix cream with spinach, basil, garlic, salt, pepper, and tomato paste in a bowl.
3. Pour this mixture over the scallops and mix gently.
4. Divide the scallops in the Air Fryer baskets, without using the crisper plate.
5. Return the Air Fryer baskets to the Air Fryer.
6. Select the "Air Fryer" mode for Zone 1 with 390°F temperature and 13 minutes cooking time.
7. Press the "Match Cook" button to copy the settings for Zone 2.
8. Start cooking by pressing the "Start/Pause" button.
9. Serve right away.

Nutrition

- Calories: 341
- Total fat: 4 g.
- Saturated fat: 0.5 g.
- Cholesterol: 69 mg.
- Sodium: 547 mg.
- Total carbohydrates: 36.4 g.
- Fiber: 1.2 g.
- Sugar: 1 g.
- Protein: 30.3 g.

84.   Fish   Finger   Sandwich

Preparation time: 10 minutes
Cooking time: 22 minutes
Servings: 4
Ingredients

- 4 small cod fillets, skinless
- Salt and black pepper to taste
- 2 tbsp. flour
- ¼ c. dried breadcrumbs
- Spray oil
- 9 oz frozen peas
- 1 tbsp. Crème Fraiche
- 12 capers
- 1 squeeze of lemon juice
- 4 bread rolls, cut in halve

Directions

1. First coat the cod fillets with flour, salt, and black pepper.
2. Then coat the fish with breadcrumbs.
3. Divide the coated cod fish into the 2 Air Fryer baskets and spray them with cooking spray.
4. Return the Air Fryer baskets to the Air Fryer.
5. Select the "Air Fryer" mode for Zone 1 with 390°F temperature and 17 minutes cooking time.
6. Press the "Match Cook" button to copy the settings for Zone 2.
7. Start cooking by pressing the "Start/Pause" button.
8. Meanwhile, boil peas in hot water for 5 minutes until soft.
9. Then drain the peas and transfer them to the blender.
10. Add capers, lemon juice, and Crème Fraiche to the blender.
11. Blend until it makes a smooth mixture.
12. Spread the peas crème mixture on top of 2 lower halves of the bread roll, and place the fish fillets on it.
13. Place the remaining bread slices on top.
14. Serve fresh.

Nutrition

- Calories: 391 Total fat: 2.2 g.Saturated fat: 2.4 g.
- Cholesterol: 10 mg. Sodium: 276 mg.
- Total carbohydrates: 7.7 g. Fiber: 0.9 g.
- Sugar: 1.4 g. Protein: 28.8 g.

85.   Lobster Tails

Preparation time: 10 minutes
Cooking time: 18 minutes
Servings: 4
Ingredients

- 4 (4 oz.) lobster tails
- 8 tbsp. butter, melted
- 2 tsp. lemon zest
- 2 garlic cloves, grated
- Salt and black pepper ground to taste
- 2 tsp. fresh parsley, chopped
- 4 wedges lemon

Directions

1. Spread the lobster tails into Butterfly, slit the top to expose the lobster meat while keeping the tail intact.
2. Place 2 lobster tails in each of the Air Fryer baskets with their lobster meat facing up.
3. Mix melted butter with lemon zest and garlic in a bowl.
4. Brush the butter mixture on top of the lobster tails.
5. And drizzle salt and black pepper on top.
6. Return the Air Fryer baskets to the Air Fryer.
7. Select the "Air Fryer" mode for Zone 1 with 390°F temperature and 18 minutes cooking time.
8. Press the "Match Cook" button to copy the settings for Zone 2.
9. Start cooking by pressing the "Start/Pause" button.
10. Garnish with parsley and lemon wedges.
11. Serve warm.

Nutrition

- Calories: 348
- Total fat: 22.4 g.
- Saturated fat: 10.1 g.
- Cholesterol: 320 mg.
- Sodium: 350 mg.
- Total carbohydrates: 32.2 g.
- Fiber: 0.7 g.
- Sugar: 0.7 g.
- Protein: 41.3 g.

86.   Buttered Mahi

Preparation time: 10 minutes
Cooking time: 17 minutes
Servings: 4

Ingredients

- 4 (6 oz) mahi fillets
- Salt and black pepper ground to taste
- Cooking spray
- ⅔ c. butter

Directions

1. Preheat your Air Fryer Machine to 350 F.
2. Rub the mahi-mahi fillets with salt and black pepper.
3. Place 2 mahi-mahi fillets in each of the Air Fryer's Basket.
4. Return the Air Fryer baskets to the Air Fryer.
5. Select the "Air Fryer" mode for Zone 1 with 390°F temperature and 17 minutes cooking time.
6. Press the "Match Cook" button to copy the settings for Zone 2.
7. Start cooking by pressing the "Start/Pause" button.
8. Add butter to a saucepan and cook for 5 minutes until slightly brown.
9. Remove the butter from the heat.
10. Drizzle butter over the fish and serve warm.

Nutrition

- Calories: 294
- Total fat: 11.1 g.
- Saturated fat: 5.8 g.
- Cholesterol: 610 mg.
- Sodium: 749 mg.
- Total carbohydrates: 49 g.
- Fiber: 0.2 g.
- Sugar: 0.2 g.
- Protein: 23.5 g.

87.   Salmon Fillets With Fennel Salad

Preparation time: 10 minutes
Cooking time: 17 minutes
Servings: 4
Ingredients

- 2 tsp. chopped fresh flat-leaf parsley
- 1 tsp. chopped fresh thyme
- 1 tsp. salt, divided
- 4 (6 oz.) skinless center-cut salmon fillets
- 2 tbsp. olive oil
- 4 c. thinly sliced fennel
- ⅔ c. 2% reduced-Fat: Greek yogurt
- 1 garlic clove, grated
- 2 tbsp. orange juice
- 1 tsp. lemon juice
- 2 tbsp. chopped fresh dill

Directions

1. At 200°F, preheat your Air Fryer.
2. Mix ½ tsp. salt, thyme, and parsley in a small bowl.
3. Brush the salmon with oil first, then rub liberally the herb mixture.
4. Place 2 salmon fillets in each of the Air Fryer baskets.
5. Return the Air Fryer baskets to the Air Fryer.
6. Select the "Air Fryer" mode for Zone 1 with 390°F temperature and 17 minutes cooking time.
7. Press the "Match Cook" button to copy the settings for Zone 2.
8. Start cooking by pressing the "Start/Pause" button.
9. Meanwhile, mix fennel with garlic, yogurt, lemon juice, orange juice, remaining salt, and dill in a mixing bowl.
10. Serve the air fried salmon fillets with fennel salad.
11. Enjoy!

Nutrition

- Calories: 350 Total fat: 3.5 g.
- Saturated fat: 0 g.
- Cholesterol: 7 mg.
- Sodium: 94 mg.
- Total carbohydrates: 15 g.
- Fiber: 1 g.
- Sugar: 1 g.
- Protein: 32 g.

88. Sweet Salmon Fillets

Preparation time: 10 minutes
Cooking time: 17 minutes
Servings: 4
Ingredients

- 4 (6 oz.) salmon fillets
- Salt
- Freshly ground black pepper
- 4 tsp. extra-virgin olive oil
- 4 tbsp. wholegrain mustard
- 2 tbsp. packed brown sugar
- 2 garlic cloves, minced
- 1 tsp. thyme leaves

Directions

1. Rub the salmon with salt and black pepper first.
2. Whisk oil with sugar, thyme, garlic, and mustard in a small bowl.
3. Place 2 salmon fillets in each of the Air Fryer baskets and brush the thyme mixture on top of each fillet.
4. Return the Air Fryer baskets to the Air Fryer.
5. Select the "Air Fryer" mode for Zone 1 with 390°F temperature and 17 minutes cooking time.
6. Press the "Match Cook" button to copy the settings for Zone 2.
7. Start cooking by pressing the "Start/Pause" button.
8. Serve warm and fresh.

Nutrition

- Calories: 349
- Total fat: 11.9 g.
- Saturated fat: 1.7 g.
- Cholesterol: 78 mg.
- Sodium: 79 mg.
- Total carbohydrates: 12.8 g.
- Fiber: 1.1 g.
- Sugar: 20.3 g.
- Protein: 35 g.

89.   Crusted Cod Fish

Preparation time: 10 minutes
Cooking time: 13 minutes
Servings: 4
Ingredients

- 2 lbs. cod fillets
- Salt to taste
- Freshly ground black pepper to taste
- ½ c. all-purpose flour
- 1 large egg, beaten
- 2 c. panko breadcrumbs
- 1 tsp. Old Bay seasoning
- Lemon wedges, for serving
- Tartar sauce, for serving

Directions

1. Rub the fish with salt and black pepper.
2. Add flour in one shallow bowl, beat egg in another bowl, and mix panko with Old Bay in a shallow bowl.
3. First coat the fish with flour, then dip it in the egg, and finally coat it with the panko mixture.
4. Place half of the seasoned cod fish in each Air Fryer basket.
5. Return the Air Fryer baskets to the Air Fryer.
6. Select the "Air Fryer" mode for Zone 1 with 390°F temperature and 13 minutes cooking time.
7. Press the "Match Cook" button to copy the settings for Zone 2.
8. Start cooking by pressing the "Start/Pause" button.
9. Flip the fish once cooked halfway, then resume cooking.
10. Serve warm and fresh with tartar sauce and lemon wedges.

Nutrition

- Calories: 413
- Total fat: 4 g.
- Saturated fat: 8 g.
- Cholesterol: 81 mg.
- Sodium: 162 mg.
- Total carbohydrates: 13 g.
- Fiber: 2.7 g.
- Sugar: 1 g.
- Protein: 22 g.

90. Glazed Scallops

Preparation time: 10 minutes
Cooking time: 13 minutes
Servings: 12
Ingredients

- 12 scallops
- 3 tbsp. olive oil
- Black pepper and salt to taste

Directions

1. Rub the scallops with olive oil, black pepper, and salt.
2. Divide the scallops into the 2 Air Fryer baskets.
3. Return the Air Fryer baskets to the Air Fryer.
4. Select the "Air Fryer" mode for Zone 1 with 390°F temperature and 13 minutes cooking time.
5. Press the "Match Cook" button to copy the settings for Zone 2.
6. Start cooking by pressing the "Start/Pause" button.
7. Flip the scallops once cooked halfway through, and resume cooking.
8. Serve warm.

Nutrition

- Calories: 279
- Total fat: 29.7 g.
- Saturated fat: 8.6 g.
- Cholesterol: 141 mg.
- Sodium: 193 mg.
- Total carbohydrates: 13.7 g.
- Fiber: 0.4 g.
- Sugar: 1.3 g.
- Protein: 10.2 g.

91.Crusted Tilapia Fillets

Preparation time: 10 minutes
Cooking time: 17 minutes
Servings: 4
Ingredients

- ¾ c. breadcrumbs
- 1 packet dry ranch-style dressing
- 2 eggs, beaten
- 4 tilapia fillets
- Herbs and chilies to garnish

Directions

1. Thoroughly mix ranch dressing with breadcrumbs in a bowl.
2. Whisk eggs in a shallow bowl.
3. Dip each fish fillet in the egg then coat evenly with the panko mixture.
4. Set 2 coated fillets in each of the Air Fryer baskets.
5. Return the Air Fryer baskets to the Air Fryer.
6. Select the "Air Fryer" mode for Zone 1 with 390°F temperature and 17 minutes cooking time.
7. Press the "Match Cook" button to copy the settings for Zone 2.
8. Start cooking by pressing the "Start/Pause" button.
9. Serve warm with herbs and chilies.

Nutrition

- Calories: 368
- Total fat: 6 g.
- Saturated fat: 1.2 g.
- Cholesterol: 351 mg.
- Sodium: 103 mg.
- Total carbohydrates: 72.8 g.
- Fiber: 9.2 g.
- Sugar: 32.9 g.
- Protein: 7.2 g.

92.   Crispy Catfish Fillets

Preparation time: 10 minutes
Cooking time: 17 minutes
Servings: 4
Ingredients

- 4 catfish fillets
- ¼ c. Louisiana fish fry
- 1 tbsp. olive oil
- 1 tbsp. chopped parsley optional
- 1 lemon, sliced
- Fresh herbs, to garnish

Directions

1. Mix fish fry with olive oil and parsley, then liberally rub over the catfish.
2. Place 2 fillets in each of the Air Fryer baskets.
3. Return the Air Fryer baskets to the Air Fryer.
4. Select the "Air Fryer" mode for Zone 1 with 390°F temperature and 17 minutes cooking time.
5. Press the "Match Cook" button to copy the settings for Zone 2.
6. Start cooking by pressing the "Start/Pause" button.
7. Garnish with lemon slices and herbs.
8. Serve warm.

Nutrition

- Calories: 401
- Total fat: 2.2 g.
- Saturated fat: 2.4 g.
- Cholesterol: 110 mg.
- Sodium: 276 mg.
- Total carbohydrates: 25 g.
- Fiber: 1.4 g.
- Sugar: 1.4 g.
- Protein: 18.8 g.

93. Shrimp Scampi

Preparation time: 10 minutes
Cooking time: 13 minutes
Servings: 6
Ingredients

- 4 tbsp. melted butter
- 1 tbsp. lemon juice
- 1 tbsp. minced garlic
- 2 tsp. red pepper flakes
- 1 tbsp. chopped chive
- 1 tbsp. minced basil leaves
- 1 lb. defrosted shrimp

Directions

1. Toss shrimp with melted butter, lemon juice, garlic, red pepper, chives, and basil in a bowl.
2. Divide the shrimp into the 2 Air Fryer baskets.
3. Return the Air Fryer baskets to the Air Fryer.
4. Select the "Air Fryer" mode for Zone 1 with 390°F temperature and 13 minutes cooking time.
5. Press the "Match Cook" button to copy the settings for Zone 2.
6. Start cooking by pressing the "Start/Pause" button.
7. Toss the shrimp once cooked halfway through, and resume cooking.
8. Serve warm.

Nutrition

- Calories: 319
- Total fat: 19.7 g.
- Saturated fat: 18.6 g.
- Cholesterol: 141 mg.
- Sodium: 193 mg.
- Total carbohydrates: 23.7 g.
- Fiber: 0.9 g.
- Sugar: 19.3 g.
- Protein: 25.2 g.

94.   Salmon Nuggets

Preparation time: 10 minutes
Cooking time: 10 minutes
Servings: 2
Ingredients

- ⅓ c. maple syrup
- ¼ tsp. ground dried chipotle powder
- 1 pinch sea salt
- 1 ½ c. croutons
- 1 large egg
- 1 (1 lb.) skinless, center-cut salmon fillet, cut into 1 ½-inch chunks
- Cooking spray

Directions

1. Mix chipotle powder, maple syrup, and salt in a saucepan and cook on a simmer for 5 minutes.
2. Crush the croutons in a food processor and transfer them to a bowl.
3. Beat egg in another shallow bowl.
4. Season the salmon chunks with sea salt.
5. Dip the salmon in the egg then coat with breadcrumbs.
6. Divide the coated salmon chunks into the 2 Air Fryer baskets.
7. Return the Air Fryer baskets to the Air Fryer.
8. Select the "Air Fryer" mode for Zone 1 with 390°F temperature and 10 minutes cooking time.
9. Press the "Match Cook" button to copy the settings for Zone 2.
10. Start cooking by pressing the "Start/Pause" button.
11. Flip the chunks once cooked halfway through, then resume cooking.
12. Pour the maple syrup on top and serve warm.

Nutrition

- Calories: 317
- Total fat: 11.9 g.
- Saturated fat: 1.7 g.
- Cholesterol: 78 mg.
- Sodium: 79 mg.
- Total carbohydrates: 14.8 g.
- Fiber: 1.1 g.
- Sugar: 8.3 g.
- Protein: 25 g.

95.   Cedar-Plank Salmon

Preparation time: 30 minutes
Cooking time: 2 hours and 30 minutes
Servings: 6
Ingredients

- 2 tbsp. grainy mustard
- 2 tbsp. mild honey or pure maple syrup
- 1 tsp. minced rosemary
- 1 tbsp. grated lemon zest
- 1 (2 lbs.) salmon fillet with skin (1 ½-inch thick)
- Salt and pepper to taste

Directions

1. Pour water on the oven broiling board to cover it, keeping it filled.
2. Plan barbecue for direct-heat cooking over medium-hot charcoal. Open vents on the base and top of a charcoal oven broil.
3. Mix together mustard, honey, rosemary, lemon zest, and rub the fillet with salt and pepper. Spread blends on the substance side of salmon and let remain at room temperature for 15 minutes.
4. Put salmon on board, skin side down. Barbecue, secured with a cover, until salmon is simply cooked through and edges are seared, 13–15 minutes. Let salmon remain on board 5 minutes before serving.

Nutrition

- Calories: 240
- Fat: 15 g.
- Carbohydrate 0 g.
- Protein: 23 g.

96.   Grilled Coconut Shrimp with Shishito Peppers

Preparation time: 25 minutes
Cooking time: 8 minutes
Servings: 4
Ingredients

- 6 garlic cloves, finely grated
- 1 tbsp. finely grated lime zest
- ¼ c. soy sauce
- ¼ c. grapeseed or vegetable oil
- 1 lb. large shrimp, peeled, deveined
- ½ c. toasted unsweetened shredded coconut
- 8 oz. shish to peppers
- ½ c. basil leaves
- ¼ c. fresh lime juice
- Flaky sea salt

Directions

1. Mix together garlic, lime zest, soy sauce, and ¼ c. oil in a medium bowl. Add shrimp and hurl to cover. Add ½ c. of coconut and hurl again to cover. Let sit while the oven broil warms, in any event, 5 minutes and up to 30 minutes.
2. Set up the oven broil for high warmth, delicately oil grind.
3. Cautiously organize shrimp in an even layer on the mesh. oven broil, cautiously turning part of the way through, until hazy and daintily singed, about 2 minutes. A portion of the coconuts will tumble off all the while, and that is alright. Move to a serving platter.
4. oven broil peppers, turning every so often and being mindful so as not to let them fall through the mesh until delicately roasted all over about 6 minutes. Transfer to a platter with shrimp.
5. Top shrimp and peppers with basil, shower with a lime squeeze, and sprinkle with ocean salt and more coconut.

Nutrition

- Calories: 82
- Fat: 7 g.
- Carbohydrate 4 g.
- Protein: 2 g.

97.   Clams with Spicy Tomato Broth and Garlic Mayo

Preparation time: 10 minutes
Cooking time: 23 minutes
Servings: 4
Ingredients

- ½ lemon
- 5 garlic cloves, 1 whole, 4 thinly sliced
- ½ c. mayonnaise
- Kosher salt
- ¼ c. plus 3 tbsp. extra-virgin olive oil
- 2 large shallots, thinly sliced
- 1 red chili (such as Holland or Fresno), thinly sliced, or ½ tsp. crushed red pepper flakes
- 2 tbsp. tomato paste
- 2 c. cherry tomatoes
- 1 c. dry white wine
- 36 littleneck clams, scrubbed
- 6 tbsp. unsalted butter, cut into pieces
- 3 tbsp. finely chopped chives
- 4 thick slices of country-style bread

Directions

1. Set up a Foodi oven broil for medium warmth. Finely grind the zest from the lemon half into a little bowl, at that point crush in the juice. Finely grind the entire garlic clove into a bowl and blend in mayonnaise. Season garlic-mayo with salt and put in a safe spot.
2. Spot a huge cast-iron skillet on the Foodi oven broil and warmth ¼ c. of oil in a skillet. Add cut garlic, shallots, and chili and cook, mixing regularly, until simply mollified, about 2 minutes. Add tomato paste and cook, mixing frequently, until the paste turns obscure somewhat around 1 minute. Add tomatoes and a touch of salt and cook, mixing every so often, until tomatoes mellow and discharge their juices, about 4 minutes. Add wine and cook until it is nearly decreased considerably and no longer scents boozy about 3 minutes.
3. Add littleneck clams and butter to the skillet and spread. Cook until littleneck clams have opened, 6–10 minutes, contingent upon the size of mollusks and warmth level. Expel skillet from Foodi oven broil; dispose of any mollusks that do not open. Sprinkle with chives.
4. In the meantime, shower bread with the remaining 3 tbsp. of oil and season softly with salt. Barbecue until brilliant earthy colored and fresh, about 3 minutes per side.
5. Serve mollusks with toasted bread and saved garlic-mayo.

Nutrition

- Calories: 282
- Fat: 10 g.
- Carbohydrate 0 g.
- Protein: 20 g.

98. Grilled Swordfish with Tomatoes and Oregano

Preparation time: 10 minutes
Cooking time: 12 minutes
Servings: 4
Ingredients

- ½ c. plus 2 tbsp. extra-virgin olive oil, plus more for the grill
- 2 tbsp. pine nuts
- 2 (12 oz.) swordfish steaks, about 1-inch thick
- Kosher salt and freshly ground pepper
- ¼ c. red wine vinegar
- 2 tbsp. drained capers, finely chopped
- 1 tbsp. finely chopped oregano, plus 2 sprigs for serving
- ½ tsp. honey
- 2 large ripe heirloom tomatoes, halved, thickly sliced

Directions

1. Set up a Foodi oven broil for medium-high warmth; delicately oil grind. Toast pine nuts in a dry little skillet over medium warmth, shaking frequently, until brilliant, about 4 minutes. Let cool and put in a safe spot for serving.
2. Pat swordfish dry and season with salt and pepper. Place on a rimmed preparing sheet and let sit at room temperature for 15 minutes.
3. Then, whisk vinegar, drained capers, chopped oregano, honey, and ½ c. of oil in a little bowl to consolidate; put the marinade in a safe spot. Place tomatoes on a rimmed platter, covering somewhat; put in a safe spot.
4. Rub swordfish done with the remaining 2 tbsp. of oil and Foodi oven broil, undisturbed until barbecue marks show up for about 4 minutes. Cautiously turn over and cook on the other side until fish is misty entirely through about 4 minutes. Transfer to saved platter with tomatoes and top with oregano branches. Season with increasingly salt and pepper. Pour held marinade over and let sit in any event 15 minutes and if necessary, 60 minutes. To serve, disperse saved pine nuts over.

Nutrition

- Calories: 210
- Fat: 10 g.
- Carbohydrate 0 g.
- Protein: 30 g.

99.   Grilled Spiced Snapper With Mango and Red Onion Salad

Preparation time: 10 minutes
Cooking time: 30 minutes
Servings: 4
Ingredients

- 1 (5 lb.) or 2 (2 ½ lb.) head-on whole fish, cleaned
- Kosher salt
- ⅓ c. chat masala, vadouvan, or tandoori spice
- ⅓ c. vegetable oil, plus more for the grill
- 1 ripe but firm mango, peeled, cut into irregular 1 ½-inch pieces
- 1 small red onion, thinly sliced, rinsed
- 1 bunch cilantro, coarsely chopped
- 3 tbsp. fresh lime juice
- Extra-virgin olive oil
- Lime wedges (for serving)

Directions

1. Place fish on a cutting board and pat dry altogether with paper towels. With a sharp blade, make slices across on an askew along the body each 2-inch on the 2 sides, chopping right down to the bones. Season fish liberally all around with salt. Coat fish with chat masala, pressing on more if necessary. Let sit at room temperature for 20 minutes.
2. In the meantime, set up a Foodi oven broil for medium-high warmth. Clean and oil grind.
3. Shower the 2 sides of fish with staying ⅓ c. of vegetable oil to cover. Foodi oven broil fish undisturbed for 10 minutes. Lift up somewhat from one edge to check whether the skin is puffed and softly roasted and effectively discharges from the mesh. If not exactly prepared, take off alone for 1 minute more or somewhere in the vicinity and attempt once more. When it is prepared, delicately slide 2 huge metal spatulas underneath and turn over. Barbecue fish until the opposite side is daintily roasted and skin is puffed, 8–12 minutes, depending on the size of the fish. Transfer onto a platter.
4. Place mango, onion, cilantro, lime juice, and a major spot of salt in a medium bowl. Sprinkle with a touch of olive oil and cover again. Spread out a mango plate of mixed greens over fish and serve with lime wedges for pressing over.

Nutrition

- Calories: 224
- Fat: 9 g.
- Carbohydrate 17 g.
- Protein: 24 g.

100. Grilled Shrimp, Zucchini, and Tomatoes With Feta

Preparation time: 30 minutes
Cooking time: 2 hours and 30 minutes
Servings: 6
Ingredients

- 1 large garlic clove, finely grated
- 2 tsp. finely chopped oregano
- ¾ tsp. kosher salt
- ¼ tsp. crushed red pepper flakes
- 2 tbsp. olive oil, plus more for a grill basket
- 10 jumbo shrimp (about 8 oz.), peeled, deveined, tails left on
- 1 medium zucchini (about 8 oz.), sliced into ¼-inch rounds
- 1 pt. cherry tomatoes
- 2 pita pockets
- ⅓ c. crumbled Feta (about 1.5 oz.)
- **Special equipment:** A flat grill basket (about 13 ½ x 8 ½-inch)

Directions

1. Set up the Foodi oven broil for high warmth. Whisk garlic, oregano, salt, red pepper, and 2 tbsp. of oil in an enormous bowl. Add shrimp, zucchini, and tomatoes and hurl to cover.
2. Brush wires of Foodi oven broil container with oil, at that point, add shrimp mix. Place in an even layer and close container. Put barbecue container on Foodi oven broil and cook, turning regularly until shrimp are completely cooked through and zucchini and tomatoes are delicately singed about 6 minutes.
3. In the meantime, barbecue pita just until warm and toasted.
4. Transfer shrimp blend to an enormous bowl and hurl until covered with tomato juices. Place on plates and top with Feta. Serve with pita close by.

Nutrition

- Calories: 178
- Fat: 3 g.
- Carbohydrate 12 g.
- Protein: 24 g.

101.   Grilled Salmon Steaks with Cilantro-Garlic Yogurt Sauce

Preparation time: 10 minutes
Cooking time: 8 minutes
Servings: 4
Ingredients

- Vegetable oil (for the grill)
- 2 Serrano chilis
- 2 garlic cloves
- 1 c. cilantro leaves with tender stems
- ½ c. plain whole-milk Greek yogurt
- 1 tbsp. extra-virgin olive oil
- 1 tsp. honey
- 2 (12-oz.) bone-in salmon steaks
- Kosher salt

Directions

1. Set up a Foodi oven broil for medium-high warmth; oil grind. Expel and dispose of seeds from 1 chili. Purée the 2 chilis, garlic, cilantro, yogurt, oil, honey, and ¼ c. of water in a blender until smooth, season well with salt. Transfer half of the sauce to a little bowl and put it in a safe spot for serving.
2. Season salmon steaks daintily with salt. Barbecue, turning on more than one occasion until the substance is beginning to turn misty, about 4 minutes. Keep on Foodi oven broiling, turning regularly and seasoning with residual sauce, until misty completely through, about 4 minutes longer. Top with the held sauce nearby.

Nutrition

- Calories: 282
- Fat: 15 g.
- Carbohydrate 0 g.
- Protein: 34 g.

CHAPTER 8:

Poultry Recipe

102. Chicken Katsu

Preparation time: 10 minutes
Cooking time: 26 minutes
Servings: 2
Ingredients

- 1 lb. boneless chicken breast, cut in half
- 2 large eggs, beaten
- 1 ½ c. panko breadcrumbs
- Salt and black pepper ground to taste
- Cooking spray

For the sauce:

- 1 tbsp. sugar
- 2 tbsp. soy sauce
- 1 tbsp. sherry
- ½ c. ketchup
- 2 tsp. Worcestershire sauce
- 1 tsp. minced garlic

Directions

1. Mix soy sauce, ketchup, sherry, sugar, garlic, and Worcestershire sauce in a mixing bowl.
2. Keep this katsu aside for a while.
3. Rub the chicken pieces with salt and black pepper.
4. Whisk eggs in a shallow dish and spread breadcrumbs in another tray.
5. Dip the chicken in the egg mixture and coat them with breadcrumbs.
6. Place the coated chicken in the 2 Air Fryer baskets and spray them with cooking spray.
7. Return the Air Fryer baskets to the Air Fryer.
8. Select the "Air Fryer" mode for Zone 1 with 390°F temperature and 26 minutes cooking time.
9. Press the "Match Cook" button to copy the settings for Zone 2.
10. Start cooking by pressing the "Start/Pause" button.
11. Flip the chicken once cooked halfway through, then resume cooking.
12. Serve warm with the sauce.

Nutrition

- Calories: 248
- Total fat: 13 g.Saturated fat: 7 g.
- Cholesterol: 387 mg.
- Sodium: 353 mg. Total carbohydrates: 1 g.
- Fiber: 0.4 g.
- Sugar: 1 g.
- Protein: 29 g.

103. Bacon-Wrapped Chicken Thighs

Preparation time: 10 minutes
Cooking time: 28 minutes
Servings: 8
Ingredients

- ⅓ lb. thick-cut bacon
- 1 ½ lbs. boneless skinless chicken thighs
- 2 tsp. minced garlic

For the butter:

- ½ stick butter softened
- ½ minced garlic clove
- ¼ tsp. dried thyme
- ¼ tsp. dried basil
- ⅛ tsp. coarse salt
- 1 pinch black pepper, ground

Directions

1. Mix garlic, softened butter, thyme, salt, basil, and black pepper in a bowl.
2. Add butter mixture on a piece of wax paper and roll it up tightly to make a butter log.
3. Place the log in the refrigerator for 2 hours.
4. Spray one bacon strip on a piece of wax paper.
5. Place each chicken thigh on top of one bacon strip and rub it with garlic.
6. Make a slit in the chicken thigh and add 1 tsp. of butter to the chicken.
7. Wrap the bacon around the chicken thigh.
8. Repeat those same steps with all the chicken thighs.
9. Place the bacon-wrapped chicken thighs in the 2 Air Fryer baskets.
10. Return the Air Fryer baskets to the Air Fryer.
11. Select the "Air Fryer" mode for Zone 1 with 390°F temperature and 28 minutes cooking time.
12. Press the "Match Cook" button to copy the settings for Zone 2.
13. Start cooking by pressing the "Start/Pause" button.
14. Flip the chicken once cooked halfway through, and resume cooking.
15. Serve warm.

Nutrition

- Calories: 457 Total fat: 19.1 g.
- Saturated fat: 11 g. Cholesterol: 262 mg.
- Sodium: 557 mg. Total carbohydrates: 18.9 g.
- Sugar: 1.2 g.
- Fiber: 1.7 g.
- Protein: 32.5 g.

104.   Bang-Bang Chicken

Preparation time: 10 minutes
Cooking time: 20 minutes
Servings: 2
Ingredients

- 1 c. mayonnaise
- ½ c. sweet chili sauce
- 2 tbsp. Sriracha sauce
- ⅓ c. flour
- 1 lb. boneless chicken breast, diced
- 1 ½ c. panko breadcrumbs
- 2 green onions, chopped

Directions

1. Mix mayonnaise with Sriracha and sweet chili sauce in a large bowl.
2. Keep ¾ c. of the mixture aside.
3. Add flour, chicken, breadcrumbs, and remaining mayo mixture to a resealable plastic bag.
4. Zip the bag and shake well to coat.
5. Divide the chicken into the 2 Air Fryer baskets in a single layer.
6. Return the Air Fryer baskets to the Air Fryer.
7. Select the "Air Fryer" mode for Zone 1 with 390°F temperature and 20 minutes cooking time.
8. Press the "Match Cook" button to copy the settings for Zone 2.
9. Start cooking by pressing the "Start/Pause" button.
10. Flip the chicken once cooked halfway through.
11. Top the chicken with reserved mayo sauce.
12. Garnish with green onions and serve warm.

Nutrition

- Calories: 392
- Total fat: 16.1 g.
- Saturated fat: 2.3 g.
- Cholesterol: 231 mg.
- Sodium: 466 mg.
- Total carbohydrates: 3.9 g.
- Sugar: 0.6 g.
- Fiber: 0.9 g.
- Protein: 48 g.

105.   Tso's Chicken

Preparation time: 10 minutes
Cooking time: 20 minutes
Servings: 4
Ingredients

- 1 egg, large
- 1 lb. boneless, skinless chicken thighs, cut into 1 ¼-inch chunks
- ⅓ c. cornstarch, plus 2 tsp. - ¼ tsp. salt
- ¼ tsp. ground black pepper
- 7 tbsp. lower-Sodium: chicken broth
- 2 tbsp. lower-Sodium: soy sauce - 2 tbsp. ketchup - 2 tsp. sugar
- 2 tsp. unseasoned rice vinegar - 1 ½ tbsp. canola oil
- 4 chilies de árbol, chopped and seeds discarded
- 1 tbsp. chopped fresh ginger - 1 tbsp. chopped garlic
- 2 tbsp. green onion, thinly sliced
- 1 tsp. toasted sesame oil - ½ tsp. toasted sesame seeds

Directions

1. Add egg to a large bowl and beat it with a fork.
2. Add chicken to the egg and coat it well.
3. Whisk ⅓ c. of cornstarch with black pepper and salt in a small bowl.
4. Add chicken to the cornstarch mixture and mix well to coat.
5. Divide the chicken into the 2 Air Fryer baskets and spray them with cooking oil.
6. Return the Air Fryer baskets to the Air Fryer.
7. Select the "ir Fryer" mode for Zone 1 with 390°F temperature and 20 minutes cooking time.
8. Press the "Match Cook" button to copy the settings for Zone 2.
9. Start cooking by pressing the "Start/Pause" button.
10. Once done, remove the air-fried chicken from the Air Fryer.
11. Whisk 2 tsp. of cornstarch with soy sauce, broth, sugar, ketchup, and rice vinegar in a small bowl. Add chilies and canola oil into a skillet and sauté for 1 minute.
12. Add garlic and ginger, then sauté for 30 seconds.
13. Stir in cornstarch sauce and cook until it bubbles and thickens.
14. Toss in cooked chicken and garnish with sesame oil, sesame seeds, and green onion.
15. Enjoy!

Nutrition

- Calories: 321 Total fat: 7.4 g.
- Saturated fat: 4.6 g. Cholesterol: 105 mg.
- Sodium: 353 mg.Total carbohydrates: 19.4 g.
- Sugar: 6.5 g. Fiber: 2.7 g.
- Protein: 37.2 g.

106.   Chicken Wing Drumettes

Preparation time: 10 minutes
Cooking time: 47 minutes
Servings: 5
Ingredients

- 10 large chicken drumettes
- Cooking spray
- ¼ c. rice vinegar
- 3 tbsp. honey
- 2 tbsp. unsalted chicken stock
- 1 tbsp. lower-Sodium: soy sauce
- ⅜ tsp. crushed red pepper
- 1 garlic clove, chopped
- 2 tbsp. chopped unsalted roasted peanuts
- 1 tbsp. chopped fresh chives

Directions

1. Spread the chicken in the 2 Air Fryer baskets in an even layer and spray cooking spray on top.
2. Return the Air Fryer baskets to the Air Fryer.
3. Select the "Air Fryer" mode for Zone 1 with 390°F temperature and 47 minutes cooking time.
4. Press the "Match Cook" button to copy the settings for Zone 2.
5. Start cooking by pressing the "Start/Pause" button.
6. Flip the chicken drumettes once cooked halfway through, then resume cooking.
7. During this time, mix soy sauce, honey, stock, vinegar, garlic, and crushed red pepper in a suitable saucepan and place it over medium-high heat to cook on a simmer.
8. Cook this sauce for 6 minutes with occasional stirring then pours it into a medium-sized bowl.
9. Add Air fried drumettes and toss well to coat with the honey sauce.
10. Garnish with chives and peanuts.
11. Serve warm and fresh.

Nutrition

- Calories: 248 Total fat: 15.7 g.
- Saturated fat: 2.7 g.
- Cholesterol: 75 mg.
- Sodium: 94 mg.
- Total carbohydrates: 31.4 g.
- Fiber: 0.4 g.
- Sugar: 3.1 g.
- Protein: 24.9 g.

107.   Crusted Chicken Breast

Preparation time: 10 minutes
Cooking time: 28 minutes
Servings: 4
Ingredients

- 2 large eggs, beaten
- ½ c. all-purpose flour
- 1 ¼ c. panko breadcrumbs
- ⅔ c. Parmesan, grated
- 4 tsp. lemon zest
- 2 tsp. dried oregano
- Salt to taste
- 1 tsp. cayenne pepper
- Freshly ground black pepper to taste
- 4 boneless skinless chicken breasts

Directions

1. Beat eggs in one shallow bowl and spread flour in another shallow bowl.
2. Mix panko with oregano, lemon zest, Parmesan, cayenne, oregano, salt, and black pepper in another shallow bowl.
3. First coat the chicken with flour first, then dip it in the eggs and coat them with panko mixture.
4. Arrange the prepared chicken in the 2 Air Fryer baskets.
5. Return the Air Fryer baskets to the Air Fryer.
6. Select the "Air Fryer" mode for Zone 1 with 390°F temperature and 28 minutes cooking time.
7. Press the "Match Cook" button to copy the settings for Zone 2.
8. Start cooking by pressing the "Start/Pause" button.
9. Flip the half-cooked chicken and continue cooking for 5 minutes until golden.
10. Serve warm.

Nutrition

- Calories: 378
- Total fat: 21 g.
- Saturated fat: 4.3 g.
- Cholesterol: 150 mg.
- Sodium: 146 mg.
- Total carbohydrates: 7.1 g.
- Sugar: 0.1 g.
- Fiber: 0.4 g.
- Protein: 23 g.

108.   Crispy Chicken Fillets

Preparation time: 10 minutes
Cooking time: 28 minutes
Servings: 4
Ingredients

- 2 boneless chicken breasts
- ½ c. dill pickle juice
- 2 eggs - ½ c. milk
- 1 c. flour, all-purpose
- 2 tbsp. powdered sugar
- 2 tbsp. potato starch
- 1 tsp. paprika - 1 tsp. sea salt
- ½ tsp. black pepper
- ½ tsp. garlic powder
- ¼ tsp. ground celery seed ground
- 1 tbsp. extra-virgin olive oil - Cooking spray
- 4 hamburger buns, toasted
- 8 dill pickle chips

Directions

1. Set the chicken in a suitable Ziplock bag and pound it into ½ thickness with a mallet.
2. Slice the chicken into 2 halves.
3. Add pickle juice and seal the bag.
4. Refrigerate for 30 minutes approximately for marination. Whisk both eggs with milk in a shallow bowl.
5. Thoroughly mix flour with spices and sugar in a separate bowl.
6. Dip each chicken slice in egg, then in the flour mixture.
7. Shake off the excess and set the chicken pieces in the Air Fryer basket.
8. Spray the pieces with cooking oil.
9. Place the chicken pieces in the 2 Air Fryer baskets in a single layer and spray them with cooking oil.
10. Return the Air Fryer baskets to the Air Fryer.
11. Select the "Air Fryer" mode for Zone 1 with 390°F temperature and 28 minutes cooking time. Press the "Match Cook" button to copy the settings for Zone 2.
12. Start cooking by pressing the "Start/Pause" button.
13. Flip the chicken pieces once cooked halfway through, and resume cooking.
14. Enjoy with pickle chips and a dollop of mayonnaise.

Nutrition

- Calories: 351 Total fat: 4 g. Saturated fat: 6.3 g.
- Cholesterol: 360 mg. Sodium: 236 mg. Total carbohydrates: 19.1 g.
- Sugar: 0.3 g. Fiber: 0.1 g. Protein: 36 g.

109.   Chicken Potatoes Mix

Preparation time: 10 minutes
Cooking time: 22 minutes
Servings: 4
Ingredients

- 15 oz canned potatoes drained
- 1 tsp. olive oil
- 1 tsp. Lawry's seasoned salt
- ⅛ tsp. black pepper optional
- 8 oz boneless skinless chicken breast cubed
- ¼ tsp. paprika optional
- ⅜ c. Cheddar cheese, shredded
- 4 slices bacon, cooked, cut into strips

Directions

1. Dice the chicken into small pieces and toss them with olive oil and spices.
2. Drain and dice the potato pieces into smaller cubes.
3. Add potato to the chicken and mix well to coat.
4. Spread the mixture in the 2 Air Fryer baskets in a single layer.
5. Return the Air Fryer baskets to the Air Fryer.
6. Select the "Air Fryer" mode for Zone 1 with 390°F temperature and 22 minutes cooking time.
7. Press the "Match Cook" button to copy the settings for Zone 2.
8. Start cooking by pressing the "Start/Pause" button.
9. Top the chicken and potatoes with cheese and bacon.
10. Return the Air Fryer baskets to the Air Fryer.
11. Select the "Air Broil" mode for Zone 1 with 300°F temperature and 5 minutes cooking time.
12. Start cooking by pressing the "Start/Pause" button.
13. Repeat the same step for Zone 2 to broil the potatoes and chicken in the 2nd basket.
14. Enjoy with dried herbs on top.

Nutrition

- Calories: 378
- Total fat: 7 g.
- Saturated fat: 8.1 g.
- Cholesterol: 230 mg.
- Sodium: 316 mg.
- Total carbohydrates: 16.2 g.
- Sugar: 0.2 g.
- Fiber: 0.3 g.
- Protein: 26 g.

110. Air Fried Turkey Breast

Preparation time: 10 minutes
Cooking time: 46 minutes
Servings: 4

Ingredients

- 2 lb. turkey breast, on the bone with skin
- ½ tbsp. olive oil
- 1 tsp. kosher salt
- ¼ tbsp. dry poultry seasoning

Directions

1. Rub turkey breast with ½ tbsp. of oil.
2. Season both its sides with poultry seasoning and salt, then rub in the brush ½ tbsp. of oil over the skin of the turkey.
3. Divide the turkey in half and place each half in each of the Air Fryer baskets.
4. Return the Air Fryer baskets to the Air Fryer.
5. Select the "Air Fryer" mode for Zone 1 with 390°F temperature and 46 minutes cooking time.
6. Press the "Match Cook" button to copy the settings for Zone 2.
7. Start cooking by pressing the "Start/Pause" button.
8. Flip the turkey once cooked halfway through, and resume cooking.
9. Slice and serve warm.

Nutrition

- Calories: 246
- Total fat: 14.8 g.
- Saturated fat: 0.7 g.
- Cholesterol: 22 mg.
- Sodium: 220 mg.
- Total carbohydrates: 40.3 g.
- Fiber: 2.4 g.
- Sugar: 1.2 g.
- Protein: 42.4 g.

111.   Chili Chicken Wings

Preparation time: 10 minutes
Cooking time: 43 minutes
Servings: 4
Ingredients

- 8 chicken wings drumettes
- Cooking spray
- ⅛ c. low-fat buttermilk
- ¼ c. almond flour
- McCormick chicken seasoning to taste

For the Thai chili marinade:

- 1 ½ tbsp. low-Sodium: soy sauce
- ½ tsp. ginger, minced
- 1 ½ garlic cloves
- 1 green onion
- ½ tsp. rice wine vinegar
- ½ tbsp. Sriracha sauce
- ½ tbsp. sesame oil

Directions

1. Put all the ingredients for the marinade in the blender and blend them for 1 minute.
2. Keep this marinade aside. Pat dries the washed chicken and place it in the Ziplock bag.
3. Add buttermilk, chicken seasoning, and zip the bag.
4. Shake the bag well, then place it in the refrigerator for 30 minutes for marination.
5. Remove the chicken drumettes from the marinade, then dredge it through dry flour.
6. Spread the drumettes in the 2 Air Fryer baskets and spray them with cooking oil.
7. Return the Air Fryer baskets to the Air Fryer.
8. Select the "Air Fryer" mode for Zone 1 with 390°F temperature and 43 minutes cooking time.
9. Press the "Match Cook" button to copy the settings for Zone 2.
10. Start cooking by pressing the "Start/Pause" button.
11. Toss the drumettes once cooked halfway through.
12. Now brush the chicken pieces with Thai chili sauce and then resume cooking
13. Serve warm.

Nutrition

- Calories: 338 Total fat: 23.8 g.
- Saturated fat: 0.7 g. Cholesterol: 22 mg.
- Sodium: 620 mg. Total carbohydrates: 8.3 g.
- Fiber: 2.4 g.
- Sugar: 1.2 g.
- Protein: 45.4 g.

112.   Turkey Mushroom Burgers

Preparation time: 10 minutes
Cooking time: 17 minutes
Servings: 4
Ingredients

- 3 medium mushrooms
- ½ tbsp. Maggi seasoning sauce
- ½ tsp. onion powder
- ¼ tsp. salt substitute
- ¼ tsp. ground black pepper
- ½ lb. ground turkey

Directions

1. Puree washed mushrooms in a food processor until smooth.
2. Add seasoning sauce, pepper, salt, and onion powder.
3. Mix well, then add this mushroom mixture to the turkey ground.
4. Combine the mixture well, then make 5 patties out of it.
5. Place half of the patties in each of the Air Fryer baskets and spray them with cooking oil.
6. Return the Air Fryer baskets to the Air Fryer.
7. Select the "Air Fryer" mode for Zone 1 with 390°F temperature and 17 minutes cooking time.
8. Press the "Match Cook" button to copy the settings for Zone 2.
9. Start cooking by pressing the "Start/Pause" button.
10. Serve warm.

Nutrition

- Calories: 438
- Total fat: 4.8 g.
- Saturated fat: 1.7 g.
- Cholesterol: 12 mg.
- Sodium: 520 mg.
- Total carbohydrates: 58.3 g.
- Fiber: 2.3 g.
- Sugar: 1.2 g.
- Protein: 32.1 g.

113.   Brazilian Chicken

Preparation time: 10 minutes
Cooking time: 47 minutes
Servings: 4
Ingredients

- 2 tsp. cumin seeds
- 2 tsp. dried parsley
- 2 tsp. turmeric powder
- 2 tsp. dried oregano leaves
- 2 tsp. salt
- 1 tsp. coriander seeds
- 1 tsp. black peppercorns
- 1 tsp. cayenne pepper
- ½ c. lemon juice
- 4 tbsp. vegetable oil
- 3 lbs. chicken drumsticks

Directions

1. Grind cumin, parsley, salt, coriander seeds, cayenne pepper, peppercorns, oregano, and turmeric in a food processor.
2. Add this mixture to lemon juice and oil in a bowl and mix well.
3. Rub the spice paste over the chicken drumsticks and let them marinate for 30 minutes.
4. Divide the chicken drumsticks in both the Air Fryer baskets.
5. Return the Air Fryer baskets to the Air Fryer.
6. Select the "Air Fryer" mode for Zone 1 with 390°F temperature and 47 minutes cooking time.
7. Press the "Match Cook" button to copy the settings for Zone 2.
8. Start cooking by pressing the "Start/Pause" button.
9. Flip the drumsticks when cooked halfway through, then resume cooking.
10. Serve warm.

Nutrition

- Calories: 378
- Total fat: 3.8 g.
- Saturated fat: 0.7 g.
- Cholesterol: 2 mg.
- Sodium: 620 mg.
- Total carbohydrates: 13.3 g.
- Fiber: 2.4 g.
- Sugar: 1.2 g.
- Protein: 25.4 g.

114.   Classic Honey Soy Chicken

Preparation time: 5–10 minutes
Cooking time: 18 minutes
Servings: 4
Ingredients

- 4 boneless, skinless chicken bosoms cut into little pieces
- 4 garlic cloves, smashed
- 1 onion, diced
- ½ c. honey
- 2 tbsp. lime juice
- 2 tsp. sesame oil
- 3 tbsp. soy sauce
- 1 tbsp. water
- 1 tbsp. cornstarch
- 1 tsp. rice vinegar

Directions

1. In a mixing bowl, add the honey, sesame oil, lime juice, soy sauce, and rice vinegar. Combine well.
2. Take Foodi multi-cooker, arrange it over a cooking platform, and open the top lid.
3. In the pot, add the onion, chicken, and garlic; add the soy sauce mixture and stir gently.
4. Seal the multi-cooker by locking it with the Pressure Lid; ensure to keep the pressure release valve locked/sealed.
5. Select "Pressure" mode and select the High Pressure level. Then, set the timer to 15 minutes and press "Start/Stop;" it will start the cooking process by building up inside pressure.
6. At the point when the clock goes off, brisk discharge pressure by adjusting the pressure valve to the Vent. After pressure gets released, open the Pressure Lid.
7. In a bowl, mix water and cornstarch until well dissolved.
8. Select "Sear/Sauté" mode and select the Medium pressure level; add the cornstarch mixture in the pot and combine it, stir-cook for 2 minutes.
9. Serve warm.

Nutrition

- Calories: 493
- Fat: 8.5 g.
- Saturated fat: 1 g.
- Trans fat: 0 g.
- Carbohydrates: 44.5 g.
- Fiber: 5 g.
- Sodium: 712 mg.
- Protein: 41.5 g.

115.   Basil and Garlic Chicken Legs

Preparation time: 10 minutes
Cooking time: 35 minutes
Servings: 4
Ingredients

- 4 chicken legs
- 2 tsps. garlic, minced
- 1 lemon, sliced
- 2 tbsps. olive oil
- 4 tsps. basil, dried
- 1 pinch of pepper and salt

Directions

1. Preheat Foodi by squeezing the "Air Crisp" alternative and setting it to 350°F and timer to 20 minutes.
2. Coat chicken with oil using a brush and drizzle with the rest of the ingredients.
3. Transfer to Foodi Grill.
4. Add lemon slices around the chicken legs.
5. Close the oven.
6. Cook for 20 minutes.
7. Serve and enjoy!

Nutrition

- Calories: 240
- Fat: 18 g.
- Saturated fat: 4 g.
- Carbohydrates: 3 g.
- Fiber: 2 g.
- Sodium: 1,253 mg.

116.   Alfredo Chicken Apples

Preparation time: 5–10 minutes
Cooking time: 20 minutes
Servings: 4
Ingredients

- 1 large apple, wedged
- 4 tsp. chicken seasoning
- 1 tbsp. lemon juice
- ¼ c. blue cheese, crumbled
- 4 chicken breasts, halved
- ½ c. alfredo sauce
- Pepper to taste

Directions

1. Take a bowl and add chicken, season it well.
2. Take another bowl and add in apple with the lemon juice.
3. Preheat Foodi by pressing the "Grill" option and setting it to Medium and timer to 20 minutes.
4. Let it preheat until you hear a beep.
5. Arrange chicken over Grill Grate, lock lid and cook for 8 minutes, flip and cook for 8 minutes more.
6. Grill apple in the same manner for 2 minutes per side (making sure to remove chicken beforehand).
7. Serve chicken with pepper, apple, blue cheese, and alfredo sauce.
8. Enjoy!

Nutrition

- Calories: 247
- Fat: 19 g.
- Saturated fat: 6 g.
- Carbohydrates: 29 g.
- Fiber: 6 g.
- Sodium: 853 mg.
- Protein: 14 g.

117.   Chicken Bean Bake

Preparation time: 5–10 minutes
Cooking time: 20 minutes
Servings: 8
Ingredients

- ½ red bell pepper, diced
- ½ red onion, diced
- 2 (8 oz.) boneless, skinless chicken breasts cut into 1-inch cubes
- 1 tbsp. extra-virgin olive oil
- 1 c. white rice
- 2 c. shredded Cheddar cheese
- 2 c. chicken broth
- 1 (15 oz.) can black beans, rinsed and drained
- 1 (1 oz.) packet taco seasoning
- 1 (15 oz.) can corn, rinsed
- 1 (10 oz.) can roasted tomatoes with chilis
- Kosher salt
- Black pepper (ground)

Directions

1. Take Foodi multi-cooker, arrange it over a cooking platform, and open the top lid. In the pot, add the oil, select "Sear/Sauté" mode, and select Medium-High Pressure level. Press "Start/Stop." After about 4–5 minutes, the oil will start simmering.
2. Put in the chicken and mix for about 2–3 minutes to brown evenly.
3. Add the onion and bell pepper, stir-cook until softened for 2 minutes. Add the rice, tomatoes, beans, corn, taco seasoning, broth, salt, and pepper, combine well.
4. Seal the multi-cooker by locking it with the Pressure Lid; ensure to keep the pressure release valve locked/sealed.
5. Select "Pressure" mode and select the High Pressure level. Then, set the timer to 7 minutes and press "Start/Stop," it will start the cooking process by building up inside pressure.
6. When the timer goes off, quickly release pressure by adjusting the pressure valve to Vent. After pressure gets released, open the Pressure Lid. Add the cheese on top.
7. Seal the multi-cooker by locking it with the Crisping Lid; ensure to keep the pressure release valve locked/sealed.
8. Select "Broil" mode and select the High Pressure level. Then, set the timer to 8 minutes and press "Start/Stop," it will start the cooking process by building up inside pressure.
9. When the timer goes off, quickly release pressure by adjusting the pressure valve to the Vent, after pressure gets released, open the Crisping Lid.

Nutrition

- Calories: 312 Fat: 15.5 g. Saturated fat: 6 g. Trans fat: 0 g.
- Carbohydrates: 24.5 g. Fiber: 5 g. Sodium: 652 mg. Protein: 24 g.

118. Hearty Chicken Zucchini Kabobs

Preparation time: 10 minutes
Cooking time: 15 minutes
Servings: 4
Ingredients

- 1 lb. chicken breast, boneless, skinless, and cut into cubes of 2-inch
- 2 tbsps. oregano
- 2 tbsps. Greek yogurt, plain
- 4 lemons juice
- 1 red onion, quartered
- 1 zucchini, sliced
- 1 lemon zest
- ½ tsp. ground black pepper
- 4 garlic cloves, minced
- 1 tsp. sea salt
- Skewers

Directions

1. Take a mixing bowl, add the Greek yogurt, lemon juice, oregano, garlic, zest, salt, and pepper, combine them well.
2. Add the chicken and coat well, refrigerate for 1–2 hours to marinate.
3. Arrange the Grill Grate and close the lid.
4. Preheat Foodi by pressing the "Grill" option and setting it to Medium and timer to 7 minutes.
5. Take the skewers, thread the chicken, zucchini, and red onion and thread alternatively.
6. Let it preheat until you hear a beep.
7. Arrange the skewers over the Grill Grate lock lid and cook until the timer reads zero.
8. Baste the kebabs with a marinating mixture in between.
9. Take out the kebabs when it reaches 165°F.
10. Serve warm and enjoy!

Nutrition

- Calories: 277
- Fat: 15 g.
- Saturated fat: 4 g.
- Carbohydrates: 10 g.
- Fiber: 2 g.
- Sodium: 146 mg.

119.   Moroccan Roast Chicken

Preparation time: 5–10 minutes
Cooking time: 22 minutes
Servings: 4
Ingredients

- 3 tbsps. plain yogurt
- 4 skinless, boneless chicken thighs
- ½ tsp. fresh flat-leaf parsley, chopped
- 2 tsps. ground cumin
- 4 garlic cloves, chopped
- ½ tsp. salt
- 2 tsps. paprika
- ¼ tsp. crushed red pepper flakes
- ⅓ c. olive oil

Directions

1. Take your food processor and add garlic, yogurt, salt, oil, and blend well.
2. Take a mixing bowl and add chicken, red pepper flakes, paprika, cumin, parsley, garlic, and mix well.
3. Let it marinate for 2–4 hours.
4. Preheat Foodi by pressing the "Roast" option and setting it to 400°F and the timer to 23 minutes.
5. Let it preheat until you hear a beep.
6. Arrange chicken directly inside the cooking pot and lock lid, cook for 15 minutes, flip and cook for the remaining time.
7. Serve and enjoy with yogurt dip!

Nutrition

- Calories: 321
- Fat: 24 g.
- Saturated fat: 5 g.
- Carbohydrates: 6 g.
- Fiber: 2 g.
- Sodium: 602 mg.
- Protein: 21 g.

120.   Chicken Zucchini Kebabs

Preparation time: 5–10 minutes
Cooking time: 15 minutes
Servings: 4
Ingredients

- Juice of 4 lemons
- Grated zest of 1 lemon
- 1 lb. boneless, skinless chicken breasts, cut into cubes of 2-inch
- 1 tsp. sea salt
- ½ tsp. ground black pepper
- 2 tbsps. plain Greek yogurt
- ¼ c. extra-virgin olive oil
- 1 red onion, quartered
- 1 zucchini, sliced
- 4 garlic cloves, minced
- 2 tbsps. dried oregano
- Skewers

Directions

1. In a mixing bowl, add the Greek yogurt, oil, lemon juice, zest, garlic, oregano, salt, and pepper. Combine the ingredients to mix well with each other.
2. Add the chicken and coat well. Refrigerate for 1–2 hours to marinate.
3. Take Foodi Grill, arrange it over your kitchen platform, and open the top lid.
4. Arrange the Grill Grate and close the top lid.
5. Press "Grill" and select the Medium Grill function. Adjust the timer to 14 minutes and then press "Start/Stop." Foodi will start preheating.
6. Take the skewers, thread the chicken, red onion, and zucchini. Thread alternatively.
7. Foodi is preheated and ready to cook when it starts to beep. After you hear a beep, open the top lid.
8. Arrange the skewers over the Grill Grate.
9. Close the top lid and allow it to cook until the timer reads zero. Baste the kebabs with a marinating mixture in between. Cook until the food thermometer reaches 165°F.
10. Serve warm.

Nutrition

- Calories: 277 Fat: 15.5 g.
- Saturated fat: 2 g. Trans fat: 0 g.
- Carbohydrates: 9.5 g.
- Fiber: 2 g.
- Sodium: 523 mg.
- Protein: 25 g.

121.   Mexican Chicken Soup

Preparation time: 5–10 minutes
Cooking time: 15 minutes
Servings: 6
Ingredients

- 1 (14.5 oz.) can black beans, rinsed and drained
- 14 oz. canned whole tomatoes, chopped
- 5 chicken thighs, boneless, skinless
- 5 c. chicken broth
- 2 c. corn kernels
- ¼ c. Cheddar cheese, shredded
- 2 tbsp. tomato puree
- 1 tbsp. chili powder
- 1 tbsp. ground cumin
- ½ tsp. dried oregano
- 2 stemmed jalapeno peppers, cored and chopped
- 3 garlic cloves, minced
- Fresh cilantro, chopped to garnish

Directions

1. Take Foodi multi-cooker, arrange it over a cooking platform, and open the top lid.
2. In the pot, add the chicken, chicken stock, cumin, oregano, garlic, tomato puree, tomatoes, chili powder, and jalapeno peppers; stir the mixture.
3. Seal the multi-cooker by locking it with the Pressure Lid; ensure to keep the pressure release valve locked/sealed.
4. Select "Pressure" mode and select the High Pressure level. Then, set the timer to 10 minutes and press "Start/Stop;" it will start the cooking process by building up inside pressure.
5. At the point when the clock goes off, brisk discharge pressure by adjusting the pressure valve to the Vent. After pressure gets released, open the Pressure Lid.
6. Shred the chicken and include it back in the pot.
7. Select "Sear/Sauté" mode and select Medium-High Pressure level; add the beans and corn and combine, stir-cook for 4 minutes.
8. Add the cilantro and cheese on top; serve warm.

Nutrition

- Calories: 408 Fat: 15 g.
- Saturated fat: 3 g. Trans fat: 0 g.
- Carbohydrates: 31 g.
- Fiber: 9 g.
- Sodium: 548 mg.
- Protein: 34 g.

CHAPTER 9:

Side Dish

122.   Turmeric Cauliflower

Preparation time: 5 minutes
Cooking time: 25 minutes
Servings: 4
Ingredients

- 2 c. cauliflower florets
- 1 c. veggie stock
- 1 handful of cilantro, chopped.
- 2 garlic cloves, minced.
- 2 tbsp. olive oil
- 2 tsp. turmeric powder
- Salt and black pepper to the taste

Directions

1. Set the Foodi on "Sauté" mode, add the oil and heat it up, and add the garlic and cook for 1 minute. Add all the ingredients, except the cilantro, toss, set the machine on "Bake" mode, and cook at 380°F for 20 minutes.
2. Add the cilantro, toss, divide everything between plates, and serve as a side dish.

Nutrition

- Calories: 243
- Carbohydrates: 0 g.
- Fat: 9.6 g.
- Protein: 36 g.

123.   Cauliflower Mix

Preparation time: 5 minutes
Cooking time: 20 minutes
Servings: 4
Ingredients

- 1 ½ c. white cauliflower, florets separated
- 1 ½ c. purple cauliflower, florets separated
- 2 garlic cloves, minced.
- ½ c. peas
- 1 carrot, cubed.
- 2 spring onions, chopped.
- 2 and ½ tbsp. soy sauce
- 2 tbsp. olive oil
- 1 pinch of salt and black pepper

Directions

1. Set the Foodi on "Sauté" mode, add the oil and heat it up. Add the spring onions and garlic, stir and cook for 2–3 minutes.
2. Add the carrots, all the cauliflower, soy sauce, salt, pepper, and peas, toss, put the Pressure Lid on and cook on High for 8 minutes. Release the pressure naturally for 10 minutes, divide everything between plates and serve as a side dish.

Nutrition

- Calories: 243
- Carbohydrates: 0 g.
- Fat: 9.6 g.
- Protein: 36 g.

124.   Potato Salad

Preparation time: 5 minutes
Cooking time: 20 minutes
Servings: 6
Ingredients

- 2 lbs. red potatoes, scrubbed
- 1 yellow onion, chopped
- 5 bacon strips, chopped
- 2 celery stalks, chopped
- ¼ c. apple cider vinegar
- 1 c. sauerkraut
- ½ c. scallions, chopped
- ½ c. water
- 1 tbsp. mustard
- ¼ tsp. sweet paprika
- 1 tsp. sugar
- 1 pinch of salt and black pepper

Directions

1. Put the potatoes and the water in your Foodi, put the Pressure Lid on and cook on High for 5 minutes and release the pressure naturally for 10 minutes.
2. Cool down the potatoes, peel, and cut into cubes. Clean the Foodi, set it on "Sauté" mode, add the bacon, stir and cook for 5 minutes.
3. Add the onion, stir and cook for another 5 minutes. Add the vinegar, toss and cook for 1 more minute.
4. Add the potatoes and all the other ingredients, toss, cook for a couple more minutes, divide everything between plates and serve as a side dish.

Nutrition

- Calories: 243
- Carbohydrates: 0 g.
- Fat: 9.6 g.
- Protein: 36 g.

125.   Zucchini Spaghetti

Preparation time: 5 minutes
Cooking time: 5 minutes
Servings: 4
Ingredients

- 3 zucchinis, cut with a spiralizer
- 1 c. sweet peas
- 1 c. cherry tomatoes, halved
- 6 basil leaves, torn

For the pesto:

- 1 /3 c. pine nuts
- ¼ c. Parmesan cheese, grated
- ½ c. olive oil
- 3 c. basil leaves
- 2 garlic cloves
- 1 pinch of salt and black pepper

Directions

1. In a blender, mix ½ c. of oil with 3 c. of basil, garlic, pine nuts, Parmesan, salt, and pepper and pulse well. Set the Foodi on "Sauté" mode, add 1 tbsp.of oil and heat it up.
2. Add the zucchini spaghetti, peas, tomatoes, and pesto, toss, put the Pressure Lid on, and cook on High for 5 minutes. Release the pressure fast for 5 minutes, add the torn basil leaves, toss, divide everything between plates and serve as a side dish.

Nutrition

- Calories: 243
- Carbohydrates: 0 g.
- Fat: 9.6 g.
- Protein: 36 g.

126.   Garlicky Broccoli

Preparation time: 5 minutes
Cooking time: 25 minutes
Servings: 4
Ingredients

- 1 broccoli head, florets separated
- 3 garlic cloves, minced
- 2 tbsp. lemon juice
- 1 tbsp. olive oil

Directions

1. Set the Foodi on "Sauté" mode, add the oil and heat it up. Add the garlic, broccoli, and lemon juice, toss and cook for 2 minutes.
2. Put the Pressure Lid on, set the machine on High, and cook for 15 minutes. Release the pressure naturally for 10 minutes, divide between plates and serve as a side dish.

Nutrition

- Calories: 243
- Carbohydrates: 0 g.
- Fat: 9.6 g.
- Protein: 36 g.

127.   Garlic Brussels Sprouts

Preparation time: 5 minutes
Cooking time: 12 minutes
Servings: 4
Ingredients

- 1 lb. Brussels sprouts, trimmed and halved
- 2 tbsp. garlic, minced.
- 6 tsp. olive oil
- Salt and black pepper to the taste

Directions

1. In your Foodi's basket, combine all the ingredients.
2. Put the basket in the pot, set it on "Air Crisp" mode, and cook the sprouts at 400°F for 12 minutes.
3. Divide between plates and serve as a side dish.

Nutrition

- Calories: 243
- Carbohydrates: 0 g.
- Fat: 9.6 g.
- Protein: 36 g.

128.   Easy Gnocchi

Preparation time: 5 minutes
Cooking time: 30 minutes
Servings: 6
Ingredients

- 50 oz. potato gnocchi
- 10 oz. baby spinach
- ½ c. Goat cheese, crumbled
- ¼ c. Parmesan cheese, grated
- 1 /3 c. white flour
- 3 and ½ c. heavy cream
- 1 ½ c. chicken stock
- 1 pinch of salt and black pepper
- Nutmeg

Directions

1. Set the Foodi on "Sauté" mode, heat it up, add the stock, cream, flour, salt, pepper, and the nutmeg, whisk well, and cook for 8 minutes.
2. Add the spinach and the gnocchi, sprinkle the Parmesan and the goat cheese on top, set the Foodi on "Bake" mode, and cook at 325°F for 15 minutes. Divide the gnocchi between plates and serve.

Nutrition

- Calories: 243
- Carbohydrates: 0 g.
- Fat: 9.6 g.
- Protein: 36 g.

129.   Warm Potato Salad

Preparation time: 5 minutes
Cooking time: 25 minutes
Servings: 4
Ingredients

- 2 gold potatoes, cut into wedges
- 3 tbsp. heavy cream
- 1 tbsp. canola oil
- Salt and black pepper to the taste

Directions

1. Put the potatoes in the Air Crisp basket and place them in the Foodi. Set the machine on "Air Crisp" mode and cook at 400°F for 10 minutes.
2. Clean the pot and transfer the potatoes to a bowl. Set the Foodi on "Sauté" mode, add the oil and heat it up. Add potato wedges, salt, pepper, and the heavy cream, toss, cook for 10 minutes more, divide between plates, and serve as a side dish.

Nutrition

- Calories: 243
- Carbohydrates: 0 g.
- Fat: 9.6 g.
- Protein: 36 g.

130.   Baby Carrots

Preparation time: 5 minutes
Cooking time: 25 minutes
Servings: 4
Ingredients

- 1 lb. baby carrots, trimmed
- 2 tbsp. lime juice
- 2 tsp. olive oil
- 1 tsp. herbs de Provence

Directions

1. In a bowl mix all the ingredients and toss them.
2. Put the basket in the Foodi, put the carrots in the basket, set the machine on "Air Crisp," and cook at 350°F for 15 minutes.
3. Divide between plates and serve as a side dish.

Nutrition

- Calories: 243
- Carbohydrates: 0 g.
- Fat: 9.6 g.
- Protein: 36 g.

131.   Zucchini Fries

Preparation time: 5 minutes
Cooking time: 20 minutes
Servings: 4
Ingredients

- 2 small zucchinis, cut into fries
- 2 eggs, whisked
- 1 c. breadcrumbs
- ½ c. white flour
- Cooking spray
- Salt and black pepper to the taste

Directions

1. In a bowl mix the flour with salt and pepper and stir. Put breadcrumbs in another bowl and the eggs on another. Dredge the zucchinis on flour, eggs, and then breadcrumbs and put them in the Foodi's Air Crisp basket.
2. Put the basket in the machine, grease the fries with the cooking spray, set the Foodi on "Air Crisp," and cook at 400°F for 12 minutes. Divide the fries between plates and serve as a side dish.

Nutrition

- Calories: 243
- Carbohydrates: 0 g.
- Fat: 9.6 g.
- Protein: 36 g.

132.   Herbed Sweet Potatoes

Preparation time: 5 minutes
Cooking time: 25 minutes
Servings: 6
Ingredients

- 3 lbs. sweet potatoes, cut into wedges
- ½ c. Parmesan, grated
- 2 garlic cloves
- 2 tbsp. butter, melted
- ½ tsp. parsley, dried
- ¼ tsp. sage, dried
- ½ tsp. rosemary, dried
- Salt and black pepper to the taste

Directions

1. In the Foodi's baking dish, combine all the ingredients and toss. Put the Reversible Rack in the Foodi, add the baking dish inside, set the machine on "Bake" mode, and cook at 360°F for 20 minutes.
2. Divide the sweet potatoes between plates and serve as a side dish.

Nutrition

- Calories: 243
- Carbohydrates: 0 g.
- Fat: 9.6 g.
- Protein: 36 g.

133.   Veggie Side Salad

Preparation time: 5 minutes
Cooking time: 25 minutes
Servings: 4
Ingredients

- 1 eggplant, cubed
- 1 green bell pepper, chopped
- 1 bunch cilantro, chopped
- 2 garlic cloves, minced
- 1 yellow onion, chopped
- 1 tbsp. tomato sauce
- 1 tbsp. olive oil
- Salt and black pepper to the taste

Directions

1. Set the Foodi on "Sauté" mode, add the oil and heat it up. Add all the ingredients, except the cilantro, toss, put the Pressure Lid on, and cook on High for 12 minutes.
2. Release the pressure naturally for 10 minutes, divide between plates and serve as a side dish with cilantro on top.

Nutrition

- Calories: 243
- Carbohydrates: 0 g.
- Fat: 9.6 g.
- Protein: 36 g.

134.   Buttery Broccoli

Preparation time: 5 minutes
Cooking time: 30 minutes
Servings: 4
Ingredients

- 1 broccoli head, florets separated
- ½ c. chicken stock
- ½ c. Parmesan cheese, grated
- 2 garlic cloves, minced
- 1 yellow onion, chopped
- 2 tbsp. parsley, chopped
- 3 tbsp. butter
- Salt and black pepper to the taste

Directions

1. Set the Foodi on "Sauté" mode, add the butter, and melt it. Add the onion and the garlic, stir and cook for 5 minutes.
2. Add all the other ingredients except the parsley and the Parmesan, toss, set the machine on "Bake" mode, and cook at 360°F for 20 minutes. Sprinkle the cheese and the Parmesan on top, toss, divide between plates and serve as a side dish.

Nutrition

- Calories: 243
- Carbohydrates: 0 g.
- Fat: 9.6 g.
- Protein: 36 g.

135. Sumac Eggplant

Preparation time: 5 minutes
Cooking time: 25 minutes
Servings: 6
Ingredients

- 2 lbs. eggplant, cubed
- 1 tbsp. olive oil
- 1 tsp. sumac
- 1 tsp. garlic powder
- Juice of 1 lime

Directions

1. Set the Foodi on "Sauté" mode, add the oil and heat it up. Add the eggplant, garlic powder, sumac, and lime juice, toss, put the Pressure Lid on, and cook on High for 15 minutes.
2. Release the pressure naturally for 10 minutes, divide the eggplant mix between plates and serve as a side dish.

Nutrition

- Calories: 243
- Carbohydrates: 0 g.
- Fat: 9.6 g.
- Protein: 36 g.

136.   Thyme Red Potatoes

Preparation time: 5 minutes
Cooking time: 35 minutes
Servings: 4
Ingredients

- 4 red potatoes, thinly sliced
- 1 tbsp. olive oil
- 2 tsp. thyme; chopped.
- Salt and black pepper the taste

Directions

1. In a bowl mix all the ingredients, toss them, and transfer them to the Air Crisp basket.
2. Put the basket in the Foodi, set the machine on "Air Crisp," and cook at 370°F for 30 minutes. Divide the potatoes between plates and serve as a side dish.

Nutrition

- Calories: 243
- Carbohydrates: 0 g.
- Fat: 9.6 g.
- Protein: 36 g.

137.   Fried Beef Dumplings

Preparation time: 45 minutes
Cooking time: 1 hour
Servings: 8

Ingredients

- 8 oz. ground beef
- 20 wonton wrappers
- 1 carrot, grated
- 1 large egg, beaten
- 1 garlic clove, minced
- ½ c. grated cabbage
- 2 tbsps. olive oil
- 2 tbsps. coconut aminos
- ½ tbsp. melted ghee
- ½ tbsp. ginger powder
- ½ tsp. salt
- ½ tsp. freshly ground black pepper

Directions

1. Put the Crisping Basket in the pot. Close the Crisping Lid, Choose the "Air Crisp," set the temperature to 400°F, and the time to 5 minutes. Press the "Start/Stop" button. In a large bowl, mix the beef, cabbage, carrot, egg, garlic, coconut aminos, ghee, ginger, salt, and black pepper.
2. Put the wonton wrappers on a clean flat surface and spoon 1 tbsp. of the beef mixture into the middle of each wrapper.
3. Run the edges of the wrapper with a little water; fold the wrapper to cover the filling into a semi-circle shape and pinch the edges to seal. Brush the dumplings with olive oil.
4. Lay the dumplings in the preheated basket, Choose the "Air Crisp," set the temperature to 400°F, and set the time to 12 minutes. Choose "Start/Stop" to begin frying.

Nutrition

- Calories: 479
- Carbohydrates: 5.2 g.
- Fat: 32.5 g.
- Protein: 0.2 g.

138.   Buttery Chicken Meatballs

Preparation time: 90 minutes
Cooking time: 2 hours
Servings: 6
Ingredients

- 1 lb. ground chicken
- 1 green bell pepper, minced
- 1 egg
- 2 celery stalks, minced
- ¼ c. hot sauce
- ½ c. water
- ¼ c. panko breadcrumbs
- ¼ c. crumbled queso fresco
- 2 tbsps. melted butter

Directions

1. Choose "Sear/Sauté" on the pot and set it to High. Choose "Start/Stop" to preheat the pot. Meanwhile, in a bowl, evenly combine the chicken, bell pepper, celery, queso fresco, hot sauce, breadcrumbs, and egg. Form meatballs from of the mixture.
2. Then, pour the melted butter into the pot and fry the meatballs in batches until lightly browned on all sides. Use a slotted spoon to remove the meatballs onto a plate.
3. Put the Crisping Basket in the pot. Pour in the water and put all the meatballs in the basket. Seal the Pressure Lid, choose "Pressure," set to High, and set the timer to 5 minutes. Choose "Start/Stop" to begin cooking.
4. When cooking is done, perform a quick pressure release, and carefully open the lid. Close the Crisping Lid. Choose the "Air Crisp," set the temperature to 360°F, and set the time to 10 minutes; press "Start."

Nutrition

- Calories: 479
- Carbohydrates: 5.2 g.
- Fat: 32.5 g.
- Protein: 0.2 g.

139.   Cheesy Smashed Sweet Potatoes

Preparation time: 30 minutes
Cooking time: 35 minutes
Servings: 4
Ingredients

- 12 oz. baby sweet potatoes
- ¼ c. shredded Monterey Jack cheese
- 1 tbsp. chopped scallions
- 1 tsp. melted butter

Directions

1. Put the Crisping Basket in the pot and close the Crisping Lid. Choose the "Air Crisp," set the temperature to 350°F, and set the time to 5 minutes. Press "Start/Stop" to begin preheating.
2. Meanwhile, toss the sweet potatoes with the melted butter until evenly coated. Once the pot and basket have preheated, open the lid and add the sweet potatoes to the basket. Close the lid, Choose the "Air Crisp," set the temperature to 350°F, and set the time to 30 minutes; press "Start."
3. After 15 minutes, open the lid, pull out the basket and shake the sweet potatoes. Return the basket to the pot and close the lid to continue cooking. When ended, check the sweet potatoes for your desired crispiness, which should also be a fork-tender texture. Top with cheese.

Nutrition

- Calories: 479
- Carbohydrates: 5.2 g.
- Fat: 32.5 g.
- Protein: 0.2 g.

140. Barbecue Chicken Drumsticks

Preparation time: 30 minutes
Cooking time: 15 minutes
Servings: 6
Ingredients

- 3 lbs. chicken drumsticks
- 1 c. Barbecue sauce
- ¼ c. butter, melted
- ½ c. water
- 3 tbsp. garlic powder
- Salt to taste

Directions

1. Season drumsticks with garlic powder and salt. Open the Foodi, pour in the water, and fit in the Reversible Rack. Arrange the drumsticks on top, close the lid, secure the pressure valve, and Select "Pressure" mode for 5 minutes. Press "Start/Stop" to start cooking.
2. Once the timer has ended, do a natural pressure release for 10 minutes, and then a quick pressure release to let out any more steam. Open the lid.
3. Remove the drumsticks to a crisp basket and add the butter and half of the barbecue sauce. Stir the chicken until well coated in the sauce.

Nutrition

- Calories: 479
- Carbohydrates: 5.2 g.
- Fat: 32.5 g.
- Protein: 0.2 g.

141.   Asparagus Wrapped in Prosciutto with Garbanzo Dip

Preparation time: 15 minutes
Cooking time: 8 minutes
Servings: 6
Ingredients

- 1 lb. asparagus, stalks trimmed
- 10 oz. Prosciutto, thinly sliced
- Cooking spray

For the dip:

- 1 medium onion, diced
- 2 medium jalapeños, chopped
- 2 cloves of garlic, minced
- 1 c. canned garbanzo beans
- 1 c. crushed tomatoes
- 1 c. vegetable broth
- 1 ½ tbsp. olive oil
- 1 tsp. paprika
- ¾ tsp. sea salt
- ½ tsp. chili powder

Directions

1. Open the Foodi and add the garbanzo beans, onion, jalapeños, garlic, tomatoes, broth, oil, paprika, chili powder, and salt. Close the lid, secure the pressure valve, and Select "Pressure" mode on High for 8 minutes. Press "Start/Stop."
2. Once the timer has ended, do a quick pressure release and open the pot.
3. Transfer the mix to a food processor, and blend until creamy and smooth. Set aside. Wrap each asparagus with a slice of prosciutto from top to bottom.
4. Grease the crisp basket with cooking spray, and add in the wrapped asparagus.

Nutrition

- Calories: 479
- Carbohydrates: 5.2 g.
- Fat: 32.5 g.
- Protein: 0.2 g.

CHAPTER 10:

Vegetables

142.   Easy Air Fried Tofu

Preparation time: 10 minutes
Cooking time: 14 minutes
Servings: 6
Ingredients

- ⅔ c. coconut aminos
- 2 (14 oz) packages extra-firm, water-packed tofu, drained
- 6 tbsp. toasted sesame oil
- ⅔ c. lime juice

Directions

1. Pat dries the tofu bars and slice into ½-inch cubes.
2. Toss all the remaining ingredients in a small bowl.
3. Marinate for 4 hours in the refrigerator. Drain off the excess water.
4. Divide the tofu cubes into the 2 Air Fryer baskets.
5. Return the Air Fryer baskets to the Air Fryer.
6. Select the "Air Fryer" mode for Zone 1 with 400°F temperature and 14 minutes cooking time.
7. Press the "Match Cook" button to copy the settings for Zone 2.
8. Start cooking by pressing the "Start/Pause" button.
9. Toss the tofu once cooked halfway through, then resume cooking.
10. Serve warm.

Nutrition

- Calories: 295
- Total fat: 3 g.
- Saturated fat: 1 g.
- Cholesterol: 283 mg.
- Sodium: 355 mg.
- Total carbohydrates: 10 g.
- Fiber: 1 g.
- Sugar: 5 g.
- Protein: 1 g.

143.   Chickpea Falafel

Preparation time: 10 minutes
Cooking time: 14 minutes
Servings: 4
Ingredients

- 1 (15.5 oz) can chickpeas, rinsed and drained
- 1 small yellow onion, cut into quarters
- 3 garlic cloves, chopped
- ⅓ c. chopped parsley
- ⅓ c. chopped cilantro
- ⅓ c. chopped scallions
- 1 tsp. cumin
- ½ tsp. kosher salt
- ⅛ tsp. crushed red pepper flakes
- 1 tsp. baking powder
- 4 tbsp. all-purpose flour
- Olive oil spray

Directions

1. Dry the chickpeas on paper towels.
2. Add onions and garlic to a food processor and chop them finely.
3. Add the parsley, salt, cilantro, scallions, cumin, and red pepper flakes.
4. Press the pulse button for 60 seconds, then toss in chickpeas and blend for 3 times until it makes a chunky paste.
5. Stir in baking powder and flour and mix well.
6. Transfer the falafel mixture to a bowl and cover to refrigerate for 3 hours.
7. Make 12 balls ftom the falafel mixture.
8. Place 6 falafels in each of the Air Fryer baskets and spray them with oil.
9. Return the Air Fryer baskets to the Air Fryer.
10. Select the "Air Fryer" mode for Zone 1 with 350°F temperature and 14 minutes cooking time.
11. Press the "Match Cook" button to copy the settings for Zone 2.
12. Start cooking by pressing the "Start/Pause" button.
13. Toss the falafel once cooked halfway through, and resume cooking.
14. Serve warm.

Nutrition

- Calories: 253 Total fat: 8.9 g.
- Saturated fat: 4.5 g. Cholesterol: 57 mg.
- Sodium: 340 mg.Total carbohydrates: 24.7 g.
- Fiber: 1.2 g. Sugar: 11.3 g.
- Protein: 5.3 g.

144.   Gingered Carrots

Preparation time: 10 minutes
Cooking time: 25 minutes
Servings: 2
Ingredients

- 1 lb. c. carrots, cut into chunks
- 1 tbsp. sesame oil
- ½ tbsp. minced ginger
- ½ tbsp. soy sauce
- ½ tsp. minced garlic
- ½ tbsp. chopped scallions, for garnish
- ½ tsp. sesame seeds for garnish

Directions

1. Toss all the ginger carrots ingredients, except the sesame seeds and scallions, in a suitable bowl.
2. Divide the carrots in the 2 Air Fryer baskets in a single layer.
3. Return the Air Fryer baskets to the Air Fryer.
4. Select the "Air Fryer" mode for Zone 1 with 390°F temperature and 25 minutes cooking time.
5. Press the "Match Cook" button to copy the settings for Zone 2.
6. Start cooking by pressing the "Start/Pause" button.
7. Toss the carrots once cooked halfway through.
8. Garnish with sesame seeds and scallions.
9. Serve warm.

Nutrition

- Calories: 327
- Total fat: 31.1 g.
- Saturated fat: 4.2 g.
- Cholesterol: 123 mg.
- Sodium: 86 mg.
- Total carbohydrates: 49 g.
- Sugar: 12.4 g.
- Fiber: 1.8 g.
- Protein: 13.5 g.

145.   Zucchini Fritters

Preparation time: 10 minutes
Cooking time: 17 minutes
Servings: 4
Ingredients

- 2 medium zucchinis, grated
- 1 c. corn kernel
- 1 medium potato cooked
- 2 tbsp. chickpea flour
- 2 garlic finely minced
- 2 tsp. olive oil
- Salt and black pepper

For the servings:

- Yogurt tahini sauce

Directions

1. Mix grated zucchinis with 1 pinch of salt in a colander and leave them for 15 minutes.
2. Squeeze out their excess water.
3. Mash the cooked potato in a large-sized bowl with a fork.
4. Add zucchini, corn, garlic, chickpea flour, salt, and black pepper to the bowl.
5. Mix the fritters' ingredients together and make balls of the size of 2 tbsp. out of this mixture and flatten them lightly.
6. Divide the fritters in the 2 Air Fryer baskets in a single layer and spray them with cooking oil.
7. Return the Air Fryer baskets to the Air Fryer.
8. Select the "Air Fryer" mode for Zone 1 with 390°F temperature and 17 minutes cooking time.
9. Press the "Match Cook" button to copy the settings for Zone 2.
10. Start cooking by pressing the "Start/Pause" button.
11. Flip the fritters once cooked halfway through, then resume cooking.
12. Serve.

Nutrition

- Calories: 398
- Total fat: 13.8 g.
- Saturated fat: 5.1 g.
- Cholesterol: 200 mg.
- Sodium: 272 mg.
- Total carbohydrates: 33.6 g.
- Fiber: 1 g.
- Sugar: 9.3 g.
- Protein: 1.8 g.

146.   Quinoa Burger

Preparation time: 10 minutes
Cooking time: 13 minutes
Servings: 4
Ingredients

- 1 c. quinoa red, white, or multi-colored
- 1 ½ c. water - 1 tsp. salt
- Black pepper, ground
- 1 ½ c. rolled oats - 3 eggs beaten
- ¼ c. minced white onion
- ½ c. crumbled Feta cheese
- ¼ c. chopped fresh chives
- Salt and ground black pepper, to taste
- Vegetable or canola oil
- 4 hamburger buns - 4 arugulas
- 4 slices tomato sliced

For the cucumber yogurt dill sauce:

- 1 c. cucumber, diced - 1 c. Greek yogurt
- 2 tsp. lemon juice - ¼ tsp. salt
- Black pepper, ground
- 1 tbsp. chopped fresh dill - 1 tbsp. olive oil

Directions

1. Add quinoa to a saucepan filled with cold water, salt, and black pepper and place it over medium-high heat. Cook the quinoa to a boil then reduce the heat, cover and cook for 20 minutes on a simmer. Fluff and mix the cooked quinoa with a fork and remove it from the heat. Spread the quinoa in a baking stay.
2. Mix eggs, oats, onion, herbs, cheese, salt, and black pepper.
3. Stir in quinoa then mix well. Make 4 patties from this quinoa cheese mixture.
4. Divide the patties into the 2 Air Fryer baskets and spray them with cooking oil.
5. Return the Air Fryer baskets to the Air Fryer.
6. Select the "Air Fryer" mode for Zone 1 with 390°F temperature and 13 minutes cooking time. Press the "Match Cook" button to copy the settings for Zone 2.
7. Start cooking by pressing the "Start/Pause" button.
8. Flip the patties once cooked halfway through, and resume cooking.
9. Meanwhile, prepare the cucumber yogurt dill sauce by mixing all of its ingredients in a mixing bowl. Place each quinoa patty in a burger bun along with arugula leaves and tomato slices. Serve with yogurt dill sauce.

Nutrition

- Calories: 361 Total fat: 15 g. Saturated fat: 7 g. Cholesterol: 46 mg.
- Sodium: 108 mg. Total carbohydrates: 33 g. Fiber: 1 g. Sugar: 26 g. Protein: 4 g.

147.   Air Fried Okra

Preparation time: 10 minutes
Cooking time: 13 minutes
Servings: 2
Ingredients

- ½ lb. okra pods sliced
- 1 tsp. olive oil
- ¼ tsp. salt
- ⅛ tsp. ground black pepper

Directions

1. Preheat your Air Fryer Machine to 350°F.
2. Toss okra with olive oil, salt, and black pepper in a bowl.
3. Spread the okra in a single layer in the 2 Air Fryer baskets.
4. Return the Air Fryer baskets to the Air Fryer.
5. Select the "Air Fryer" mode for Zone 1 with 375°F temperature and 13 minutes cooking time.
6. Press the "Match Cook" button to copy the settings for Zone 2.
7. Start cooking by pressing the "Start/Pause" button.
8. Toss the okra once cooked halfway through, and resume cooking.
9. Serve warm.

Nutrition

- Calories: 188
- Total fat: 1 g.
- Saturated fat: 7 g.
- Cholesterol: 136 mg.
- Sodium: 128 mg.
- Total carbohydrates: 15 g.
- Fiber: 1 g.
- Sugar: 26 g.
- Protein: 4 g.

148.   Hasselback Potatoes

Preparation time: 10 minutes
Cooking time: 25 minutes
Servings: 4
Ingredients

- 4 medium Yukon Gold potatoes
- 3 tbsp. melted butter
- 1 tbsp. olive oil
- 3 garlic cloves, crushed
- ½ tsp. ground paprika
- Salt and black pepper ground, to taste
- 1 tbsp. chopped fresh parsley

Directions

1. Slice each potato from the top to make ¼-inch slices, without cutting its ½-inch bottom, keeping the potato's bottom intact.
2. Mix butter, with olive oil, garlic, and paprika in a small bowl.
3. Brush the garlic mixture on top of each potato and add the mixture into the slits.
4. Season them with salt and black pepper.
5. Place 2 seasoned potatoes in each of the Air Fryer baskets.
6. Return the Air Fryer baskets to the Air Fryer.
7. Select the "Air Fryer" mode for Zone 1 with 375°F temperature and 25 minutes cooking time.
8. Press the "Match Cook" button to copy the settings for Zone 2.
9. Start cooking by pressing the "Start/Pause" button.
10. Brushing the potatoes again with butter mixture after 15 minutes then resume cooking.
11. Garnish with parsley.
12. Serve warm.

Nutrition

- Calories: 362
- Total fat: 10 g.
- Saturated fat: 9 g.
- Cholesterol: 326 mg.
- Sodium: 18 mg.
- Total carbohydrates: 48 g.
- Fiber: 1 g.
- Sugar: 2 g.
- Protein: 5 g.

149.   Roasted Spicy Potatoes

Preparation time: 15 minutes
Cooking time: 25 minutes
Servings: 4
Ingredients

- 1 lb. baby potatoes, sliced into wedges
- 2 tbsps. olive oil
- Salt to taste
- 1 tbsp. garlic powder
- 1 tbsp. paprika
- ½ c. mayonnaise
- 2 tbsps. white wine vinegar
- 2 tbsps. tomato paste
- 1 tsp. chili powder

Directions

1. Toss potatoes in oil.
2. Sprinkle with salt, garlic powder, and paprika.
3. Add crisper plate to the Air Fryer basket.
4. Add a basket to the Foodi Grill.
5. Set it to Air Fry. Set it to 360°F for 30 minutes.
6. Press "Start" to preheat.
7. Put the potatoes on the crisper plate after 3 minutes.
8. Cook for 25 minutes.
9. While waiting, mix the remaining ingredients.
10. Toss potatoes in spicy mayo mixture and serve.

Nutrition

- Calories: 178
- Fat: 10 g.
- Saturated fat: 5 g.
- Carbohydrates: 39 g.
- Fiber: 6 g.
- Sodium: 29 mg.
- Protein: 5 g.

150. Grilled Cauliflower Steak

Preparation time: 30 minutes
Cooking time: 25 minutes
Servings: 2
Ingredients

- 2 cauliflower steaks
- ¼ c. vegetable oil, divided
- Salt and pepper to taste
- 1 onion, chopped
- 3 garlic cloves, minced
- ½ c. roasted red bell peppers, chopped
- ¼ c. Kalamata olives, chopped
- 1 tbsp. fresh parsley, chopped
- 1 tbsp. fresh oregano, chopped
- ½ lb. Feta cheese, crumbled
- 1 tbsp. lemon juice
- 1 /4 c. walnuts, chopped

Directions

1. Add the Grill Grate to your Foodi Grill.
2. Choose the "Grill" setting.
3. Set it to Max for 17 minutes.
4. Press "Start" to preheat.
5. Brush both sides of cauliflower steaks with oil.
6. Season with salt and pepper.
7. Grill for 10 minutes per side.
8. Mix the remaining ingredients in a bowl.
9. Spread mixture on top of the steaks and cook for another 2 minutes.

Nutrition

- Calories: 240
- Fat: 11 g.
- Saturated fat: 3 g.
- Carbohydrates: 33 g.
- Fiber: 4 g.
- Sodium: 259 mg.
- Protein: 6 g.

151.   Delicious Broccoli and Arugula

Preparation time: 10 minutes
Cooking time: 12 minutes
Servings: 4
Ingredients

- Pepper as needed
- ½ tsp. salt
- Red pepper flakes
- 2 tbsps. extra-virgin olive oil
- 1 tbsp. canola oil
- ½ red onion, sliced
- 1 garlic clove, minced
- 1 tsp. Dijon mustard
- 1 tsp. honey
- 1 tbsp. lemon juice
- 2 tbsps. Parmesan cheese, grated
- 4 c. arugula, torn
- 2 heads broccoli, trimmed

Directions

1. Preheat your Foodi Grill to Max and set the timer to 12 minutes.
2. Take a large-sized bowl and add broccoli, sliced onion, and canola oil, toss the mixture well until coated.
3. Once you hear the beep, it is preheated.
4. Arrange your vegetables over the Grill Grate, let them grill for 8–12 minutes.
5. Take a medium-sized bowl and whisk in lemon juice, olive oil, mustard, honey, garlic, red pepper flakes, pepper, and salt.
6. Once done, add the prepared veggies and arugula to a bowl.
7. Drizzle the prepared vinaigrette on top, sprinkle a bit of Parmesan.
8. Stir and mix.
9. Enjoy!

Nutrition

- Calories: 168
- Fat: 12 g.
- Saturated fat: 3 g.
- Carbohydrates: 13 g.
- Fiber: 1 g.
- Sodium: 392 mg.
- Protein: 6 g.

152. Vegetable Fritters

Preparation time: 10 minutes
Cooking time: 15 minutes
Servings: 4
Ingredients

- 3 tbsps. ground flaxseed mixed with ½ c. water
- 2 potatoes, shredded
- 2 c. frozen mixed vegetables
- 1 c. frozen peas, thawed
- ½ c. onion, chopped
- ¼ c. fresh cilantro, chopped
- ½ c. almond flour
- Salt to taste
- Cooking spray

Directions

1. Combine all the ingredients in a bowl. Form patties. Spray each patty with oil.
2. Transfer to the Foodi basket. Set it to "Air Crisp." Close the Crisping Lid.
3. Cook at 360°F for 15 minutes, flipping halfway through.

Nutrition

- Calories: 171
- Total fat: 0.5 g.
- Saturated fat: 0.1 g.
- Cholesterol: 0 mg.
- Sodium: 107 mg.
- Total Carbohydrate: 35.7 g.
- Dietary fiber: 9.1 g.
- Total sugar: 6.5 g.
- Iron: 2 mg.

153. Crazy Fresh Onion Soup

Preparation time: 5 minutes
Cooking time: 10–15 minutes
Servings: 3
Ingredients

- 2 tbsps. avocado oil
- 8 c. yellow onion
- 1 tbsp. balsamic vinegar
- 6 c. pork stock
- 1 tsp. salt
- 2 bay leaves
- 2 large sprigs, fresh thyme

Directions

1. Cut up the onion in half through the root.
2. Peel them and slice into thin half-moons.
3. Set the pot to "Sauté" mode and add oil. Once the oil is hot, add the onions.
4. Cook for about 15 minutes.
5. Add balsamic vinegar and scrape any fond from the bottom.
6. Add stock, bay leaves, salt, and thyme.
7. Lock up the lid and cook on High Pressure for 10 minutes.
8. Release the pressure naturally.
9. Discard the bay leaf and thyme stems.
10. Blend the soup using an immersion blender and serve!

Nutrition

- Calories: 454
- Fat: 31 g.
- Carbohydrates: 7 g.
- Protein: 27 g.

154.   Elegant Zero Crust Kale and Mushroom Quiche

Preparation time: 5 minutes
Cooking time: 9 hours
Servings: 3
Ingredients

- 6 large eggs
- 2 tbsps. unsweetened almond milk
- 2 oz. low-fat Feta cheese, crumbled
- ¼ c. Parmesan cheese, grated
- 1 ½ tsps. Italian seasoning
- 4 oz. mushrooms, sliced
- 2 c. kale, chopped

Directions

1. Grease the inner pot of your Foodi.
2. Take a large bowl and whisk in eggs, cheese, almond milk, seasoning, and mix it well.
3. Stir in kale and mushrooms. Pour the mix into Foodi. Gently stir.
4. Place lid and cook on "Slow Cook" mode (low) for 8–9 hours. Serve and enjoy!

Nutrition

- Calories: 112
- Fat: 7 g.
- Carbohydrates: 4 g.
- Protein: 10 g.

155. Delicious Beet Borscht

Preparation time: 5 minutes
Cooking time: 45 minutes
Servings: 3
Ingredients

- 8 c. beets
- ½ c. celery, diced
- ½ c. carrots, diced
- 2 garlic cloves, diced
- 1 medium onion, diced
- 3 c. cabbage, shredded
- 6 c. beef stock
- 1 bay leaf
- 1 tbsp. salt
- ½ tbsp. thyme
- ¼ c. fresh dill, chopped
- ½ c. coconut yogurt

Directions

1. Add the washed beets to a steamer in the Foodi.
2. Add 1 c. water. Steam for 7 minutes.
3. Perform a quick release and drop into an ice bath.
4. Carefully peel off the skin and dice the beets.
5. Transfer the diced beets, celery, carrots, onion, garlic, cabbage, stock, bay leaf, thyme, and salt to your Instant Pot. Lock up the lid and set the pot to "Soup" mode, cook for 45 minutes.
6. Release the pressure naturally. Transfer to bowls and top with a dollop of dairy-free yogurt.
7. Enjoy with a garnish of fresh dill!

Nutrition

- Calories: 625
- Fat: 46 g.
- Carbohydrates: 19 g.
- Protein: 90 g.

156.   Pepper Jack Cauliflower Meal

Preparation time: 5 minutes
Cooking time: 3 hours and 35 minutes
Servings: 3
Ingredients

- 1 head cauliflower
- ¼ c. whipping cream
- 4 oz. cream cheese
- ½ tsp. pepper
- 1 tsp. salt
- 2 tbsps. butter
- 4 oz. pepper jack cheese
- 6 bacon slices, crumbled

Directions

1. Grease the Foodi and add listed ingredients (except cheese and bacon).
2. Stir and lock the lid, cook on "Slow Cook" mode (low) for 3 hours.
3. Remove lid and add cheese, stir. Lock the lid again and cook for 1 hour more.
4. Garnish with bacon crumbles and enjoy!

Nutrition

- Calories: 272
- Fat: 21 g.
- Carbohydrates: 5 g.
- Protein: 10 g.

THE COMPLETE FOODI 2-BASKET AIR FRYER COOKBOOK 2021

157.   Slow-Cooked Brussels

Preparation time: 5 minutes
Cooking time: 5 hours
Servings: 3
Ingredients

- 1 lb. Brussel sprouts, bottom trimmed and cut
- 1 tbsp. olive oil
- 1 ½ tbsp. Dijon mustard
- ¼ c. water
- Salt and pepper as needed
- ½ tsp. dried tarragon

Directions

1. Add Brussel sprouts, salt, water, pepper, and olive oil to the Foodi.
2. Add dried tarragon and stir.
3. Lock the lid and cook on "Slow Cook" mode (low) for 5 hours until the sprouts are tender.
4. Stir well and add Dijon mustard over sprouts. Stir and enjoy!

Nutrition

- Calories: 83
- Fat: 4 g.
- Carbohydrates: 11 g.
- Protein: 4 g.

186 | P a g .

158.   Honey Dressed Asparagus

Preparation time: 5–10 minutes
Cooking time: 15 minutes
Servings: 4
Ingredients

- 2 lbs. asparagus, trimmed
- 4 tbsps. tarragon, minced
- ¼ c. honey
- 2 tbsps. olive oil
- 1 tsp. salt
- ½ tsp. pepper

Directions

1. Add asparagus, oil, salt, honey, pepper, tarragon into your bowl. Toss them well.
2. Preheat your Foodi by pressing the "Grill" option and setting it to Medium.
3. Set the timer to 8 minutes.
4. Allow it to preheat until you hear a beep sound.
5. Arrange asparagus over Grill Grate and lock the lid.
6. Cook for 4 minutes.
7. Then flip asparagus and cook for 4 minutes more.
8. Serve and enjoy!

Nutrition

- Calories: 240
- Fat: 15 g.
- Saturated fat: 3 g.
- Carbohydrates: 31 g.
- Fiber: 1 g.
- Sodium: 103 mg.
- Protein: 7 g.

159.   Italian Squash Meal

Preparation time: 5–10 minutes
Cooking time: 16 minutes
Servings: 4

Ingredients

- 1 medium butternut squash, peeled, seeded, and cut into ½-inch slices
- 1 ½ tsps. oregano, dried
- 1 tsp. dried thyme
- 1 tbsp. olive oil
- ½ tsp. salt
- ¼ tsp. black pepper

Directions

1. Add slices alongside the other ingredients into a mixing bowl.
2. Mix them well.
3. Preheat your Foodi by pressing the "Grill" option and setting it to Medium.
4. Set the timer to 16 minutes.
5. Allow it to preheat until it beeps.
6. Arrange squash slices over the Grill Grate.
7. Cook for 8 minutes.
8. Flip and cook for 8 minutes more.
9. Serve and enjoy!

Nutrition

- Calories: 238
- Fat: 12 g.
- Saturated fat: 2 g.
- Carbohydrates: 36 g.
- Fiber: 3 g.
- Sodium: 128 mg.
- Protein: 15 g.

160.   Air Grilled Brussels

Preparation time: 5–10 minutes
Cooking time: 12 minutes
Servings: 4
Ingredients

- 6 slices bacon, chopped
- 1 lb. Brussels sprouts halved
- 2 tbsps. extra-virgin olive oil
- 1 tsp. salt
- ½ tsp. black pepper, ground

Directions

1. Add Brussels, olive oil, salt, pepper, and bacon into a mixing bowl.
2. Preheat the Foodi by pressing the "Air Crisp" option and setting it to 390°F.
3. Set the timer to 12 minutes.
4. Allow it to preheat until it beeps.
5. Arrange Brussels over the basket and lock the lid.
6. Cook for 6 minutes.
7. Shake it and cook for 6 minutes more.
8. Serve and enjoy!

Nutrition

- Calories: 279
- Fat: 18 g.
- Saturated fat: 4 g.
- Carbohydrates: 12 g.
- Fiber: 4 g.
- Sodium: 874 mg.

161.   Slowly Cooked Lemon Artichokes

Preparation time: 10 minutes
Cooking time: 5 hours
Servings: 4
Ingredients

- 5 large artichokes
- 1 tsp. sea salt
- 2 stalks celery, sliced
- 2 large carrots, cut into matchsticks
- Juice from ½ a lemon
- ¼ tsp. black pepper
- 1 tsp. dried thyme
- 1 tbsp. dried rosemary
- Lemon wedges for garnish

Directions

1. Remove the stalk from your artichokes and remove the tough outer shell.
2. Transfer the chokes to your Foodi and add 2 c. boiling water.
3. Add celery, lemon juice, salt, carrots, black pepper, thyme, and rosemary.
4. Cook on "Slow Cook" mode (high) for 4–5 hours.
5. Serve the artichokes with lemon wedges. Serve and enjoy!

Nutrition

- Calories: 205
- Fat: 2 g.
- Carbohydrates: 12 g.
- Protein: 34 g.

CHAPTER 11:

Desserts

162.   Peanut Butter Cups

Preparation time: 15 minutes
Cooking time: 30 minutes
Servings: 3
Ingredients

- 1 c. butter
- ¼ c. heavy cream
- 2 oz. unsweetened chocolate
- ¼ c. peanut butter, separated
- 4 packets Stevia

Directions

1. Melt the peanut butter and butter in a bowl and stir well with unsweetened chocolate, Stevia, and cream.
2. Mix well and pour the mixture into a baking mold.
3. Put the baking mold in the Foodi and press "Bake/Roast."
4. Set the timer for 30 minutes at 360°F and dish out to serve.

Nutrition

- Calories: 479
- Total fat: 51.5 g.
- Saturated fat: 29.7 g.
- Cholesterol: 106 mg.
- Sodium: 69 mg.
- Total carbohydrates: 7.7 g.
- Fiber: 2.7 g.
- Sugar: 1.4 g.
- Protein: 5.2 g.

163.   Chocolate Brownies

Preparation time: 15 minutes
Cooking time: 32 minutes
Servings: 4
Ingredients

- 3 eggs
- ½ c. butter
- ½ c. sugar-free chocolate chips
- 2 scoops Stevia
- 1 tsp. vanilla extract

Directions

1. In a bowl, mix eggs, Stevia, and vanilla extract.
2. Pour this mixture into the blender and blend until smooth.
3. Put the butter and chocolate in the pot of Foodi and press sauté.
4. Sauté for 2 minutes until the chocolate is melted.
5. Add the melted chocolate into the egg mixture.
6. Pour the mixture into the baking mold and place it in the Foodi.
7. Press "Bake/Roast" and set the timer for about 30 minutes at 360°F.
8. Bake for about 30 minutes, cut into pieces and serve.

Nutrition

- Calories: 266
- Total fat: 26.9 g.
- Saturated fat: 15.8 g.
- Cholesterol: 184 mg.
- Sodium: 218 mg.
- Total carbohydrates: 2.5 g.
- Fiber: 0 g.
- Sugar: 0.4 g.
- Protein: 4.5 g.

164.   Cream Crepes

Preparation time: 15 minutes
Cooking time: 4 minutes
Servings: 6
Ingredients

- 1 ½ tsps. Splenda
- 3 organic eggs
- 3 tbsps. coconut flour
- ½ c. heavy cream
- 3 tbsps. coconut oil, melted and divided
- Salt to taste

Directions

1. In a bowl, mix 1 ½ tbsps. of coconut oil, Splenda, eggs, and salt.
2. Add the coconut flour and continuously stir.
3. Add the heavy cream and stir continuously until smooth.
4. Press sauté on Foodi and pour about ¼ of the mixture in the pot.
5. Sauté for 2 minutes on each side and dish out.
6. Repeat until the mixture ends and serve.

Nutrition

- Calories: 145
- Total fat: 13.1 g.
- Saturated fat: 9.1 g.
- Cholesterol: 96 mg.
- Sodium: 35 mg.
- Total carbohydrates: 4 g.
- Fiber: 1.5 g.
- Sugar: 1.2 g.
- Protein: 3.5 g.

165.   Nut Porridge

Preparation time: 15 minutes
Cooking time: 10 minutes
Servings: 4
Ingredients

- 4 tsps. coconut oil, melted
- 1 c. pecans, halved
- 2 c. water
- 2 tbsps. Stevia
- 1 c. cashew nuts, raw and unsalted

Directions

1. Put the cashew nuts and pecans in the precision processor and pulse till they are in chunks.
2. Put this mixture into the pot of Foodi and stir in water, coconut oil, and Stevia.
3. Select "Sauté" on Foodi and cook for 15 minutes.
4. Serve and enjoy.

Nutrition

- Calories: 260
- Total fat: 22.9 g.
- Saturated fat: 7.3 g.
- Cholesterol: 0 mg.
- Sodium: 9 mg.
- Total carbohydrates: 12.7 g.
- Fiber: 1.4 g.
- Sugar: 1.8 g.
- Protein: 5.6 g.

166.   Lemon Mousse

Preparation time: 15 minutes
Cooking time: 12 minutes
Servings: 2
Ingredients

- 4 oz. cream cheese softened
- ½ c. heavy cream
- ⅛ c. fresh lemon juice
- ½ tsp. lemon liquid Stevia
- 2 pinches salt

Directions

1. In a bowl, mix cream cheese, heavy cream, lemon juice, salt, and Stevia.
2. Pour this mixture into the ramekins and transfer the ramekins into the pot of Foodi.
3. Select "Bake/Roast" and bake for 12 minutes at 350°F.
4. Pour into the serving glasses and refrigerate for at least 3 hours.

Nutrition

- Calories: 305
- Total fat: 31 g.
- Saturated fat: 19.5 g.
- Cholesterol: 103 mg.
- Sodium: 299 mg.
- Total carbohydrates: 2.7 g.
- Fiber: 0.1 g.
- Sugar: 0.5 g.
- Protein: 5 g.

167.   Chocolate Cheesecake

Preparation time: 15 minutes
Cooking time: 15 minutes
Servings: 6
Ingredients

- 2 c. cream cheese, softened
- 2 eggs
- 2 tbsps. cocoa powder
- 1 tsp. pure vanilla extract
- ½ c. Swerve

Directions

1. Add eggs, cocoa powder, vanilla extract, swerve, cream cheese in an immersion blender and blend until smooth.
2. Pour the mixture evenly into mason jars.
3. Put the mason jars into the insert of Foodi and close the lid.
4. Select "Bake/Roast" and bake for 15 minutes at 360°F.
5. Refrigerate for at least 2 hours.

Nutrition

- Calories: 244
- Total fat: 24.8 g.
- Saturated fat: 15.6 g.
- Cholesterol: 32 mg.
- Sodium: 204 mg.
- Total carbohydrates: 2.1 g.
- Fiber: 0.1 g.
- Sugar: 0.4 g.
- Protein: 4 g.

168.   Vanilla Yogurt

Preparation time: 15 minutes
Cooking time: 4 hours
Servings: 2
Ingredients

- ½ cup full-Fat: milk
- ¼ cup yogurt starter
- 1 cup heavy cream
- ½ tbsp. pure vanilla extract
- 2 scoops Stevia

Directions

1. Add milk, heavy cream, vanilla extract, and Stevia in Foodi.
2. Let yogurt sit and press "Slow Cook" and set the timer to 4 hours on Low.
3. Add yogurt starter in 1 c. of milk.
4. Return this mixture to the pot.
5. Close the lid and wrap the Foodi in small towels.
6. Let yogurt sit for about 9 hours.
7. Dish out, refrigerate and then serve.

Nutrition

- Calories: 292
- Total fat: 26.2 g.
- Saturated fat: 16.3 g.
- Cholesterol: 100 mg.
- Sodium: 86 mg.
- Total carbohydrates: 8.2 g.
- Fiber: 0 g.
- Sugar: 6.6 g.
- Protein: 5.2 g.

169.   Coffee Custard

Preparation time: 15 minutes
Cooking time: 10 minutes
Servings: 4
Ingredients

- 4 oz. mascarpone cream cheese
- 1 tsp. espresso powder
- ¼ c. unsalted butter
- 4 large organic eggs, whites and yolks separated
- 1 tbsp. water
- ¼ tsp. cream of tartar
- ½ tsp. liquid Stevia
- ¼ tsp. monk fruit extract drops

Directions

1. Select "Sauté" and Low-Medium on Foodi and add butter and cream cheese, sauté for 3 minutes and mix in espresso powder, egg yolks, and water.
2. Put it on Low and cook for 4 minutes.
3. In a bowl, whisk together egg whites, fruit drops, Stevia, and cream of tartar.
4. Pour in the egg white mixture in the mixture present in Foodi and cook for 3 minutes.
5. Pour it into serving glasses and refrigerate it for 3 hours.

Nutrition

- Calories: 292
- Total fat: 26.2 g.
- Saturated fat: 16.3 g.
- Cholesterol: 100 mg.
- Sodium: 86 mg.
- Total carbohydrates: 8.2 g.
- Fiber: 0 g.
- Sugar: 6.6 g.
- Protein: 5.2 g.

170. Chocolate Fudge 1

Preparation time: 15 minutes
Cooking time: 17 minutes
Servings: 24
Ingredients

- ½ tsp. organic vanilla extract
- 1 c. heavy whipping cream
- 2 oz. butter softened
- 2 oz. 70% dark chocolate, finely chopped

Directions

1. Select "Sauté" and Medium-High on Foodi and add vanilla and heavy cream, sauté for 5 minutes at Low.
2. Sauté for 10 minutes and add butter and chocolate.
3. Sauté for 2 minutes and pour this mixture into a serving dish.
4. Refrigerate it for some hours and serve.

Nutrition

- Calories: 292
- Total fat: 26.2 g.
- Saturated fat: 16.3 g.
- Cholesterol: 100 mg.
- Sodium: 86 mg.
- Total carbohydrates: 8.2 g.
- Fiber: 0 g.
- Sugar: 6.6 g.
- Protein: 5.2 g.

171.   Lime Cheesecake

Preparation time: 15 minutes
Cooking time: 30 minutes
Servings: 6
Ingredients

- ¼ c. Erythritol, plus 1 tsp.
- 8 oz. cream cheese, softened
- ⅓ c. Ricotta cheese
- 1 tsp. fresh lime zest, grated
- 2 tbsps. fresh lime juice
- ½ tsp. organic vanilla extract
- 2 organic eggs
- 2 tbsps. sour cream

Directions

1. In a bowl, add ¼ c. Erythritol and the remaining ingredients, except for the eggs and the sour cream, and with a hand mixer beat on high speed until smooth.
2. Add the eggs and beat on low speed until well combined.
3. Transfer the mixture into a 6-inch greased springform pan evenly.
4. With a piece of foil, cover the pan.
5. In the pot of Foodi, place 2 c. of water.
6. Arrange a Reversible Rack in the pot of Foodi.
7. Place the springform pan over the Reversible Rack.
8. Close the Foodi with the Pressure Lid and place the pressure valve into the "Seal" position.
9. Select "Pressure" and set it to High for 30 minutes.
10. Press "Start/Stop" to begin cooking.
11. Switch the valve to Vent and do a natural release.
12. Place the pan onto a wire rack to cool slightly.
13. Meanwhile, in a small bowl, add the sour cream and remaining Erythritol and beat until well combined.
14. Spread the cream mixture on the warm cake evenly.
15. Refrigerate for about 6–8 hours before serving.

Nutrition

- Calories: 182 Fat: 16.6 g.
- Net carbohydrates: 2.1 g.
- Carbohydrates: 2.1 g.
- Fiber: 0 g.
- Sugar: 0.3 g.
- Protein: 6.4 g.
- Sodium: 152 mg.

172.   Lemon Cheesecake

Preparation time: 15 minutes
Cooking time: 4 hours
Servings: 12
Ingredients
For the crust:

- 1 ½ c. almond flour
- 4 tbsps. butter, melted
- 3 tbsps. sugar-free peanut butter
- 3 tbsps. Erythritol
- 1 large organic egg, beaten

For the filling:

- 1 c. Ricotta cheese
- 24 oz. cream cheese, softened
- 1 ½ c. Erythritol
- 2 tsps. liquid Stevia
- ⅓ c. heavy cream
- 2 large organic eggs
- 3 large organic egg yolks
- 1 tbsp. fresh lemon juice
- 1 tbsp. organic vanilla extract

Directions

1. Grease the pot of Foodi.
2. For the crust: In a bowl, add all the ingredients and mix until well combined.
3. In the pot prepared of Foodi, place the crust mixture and press to smooth the top surface.
4. With a fork, prick the crust at many places.
5. For the filling: In a food processor, add the Ricotta cheese and pulse until smooth.
6. In a large bowl, add the Ricotta, cream cheese, Erythritol, and Stevia and with an electric mixer, beat over medium speed until smooth.
7. In another bowl, add the heavy cream, eggs, egg yolks, lemon juice, and vanilla extract and beat until well combined. Add the egg mixture into the cream cheese mixture and beat over medium speed until just combined. Place the filling mixture over the crust evenly.
8. Close the Foodi with the Crisping Lid and select "Slow Cook."
9. Set on low for 3–4 hours. Press "Start/Stop" to begin cooking.
10. Place the pan onto a wire rack to cool.
11. Refrigerate to chill for at least 6–8 hours before serving.

Nutrition

- Calories: 410 Fat: 37.9 g. Net carbohydrates: 5.1 g. Carbohydrates: 6.9 g.
- Fiber: 1.8 g. Sugar: 1.3 g. Protein: 13 g. Sodium: 260 mg.

173.   Strawberry Crumble

Preparation time: 15 minutes
Cooking time: 2 hours
Servings: 5
Ingredients

- 1 c. almond flour
- 2 tbsps. butter, melted
- 8–10 drops liquid Stevia
- 3–4 c. fresh strawberries, hulled and sliced
- 1 tbsp. butter, chopped

Directions

1. Lightly, grease the pot of Foodi.
2. In a bowl, add the flour, melted butter, and Stevia and mix until a crumbly mixture form.
3. In the pot of the prepared Foodi, place the strawberry slices and dot with chopped butter.
4. Spread the flour mixture on top evenly.
5. Close the Foodi with the Crisping Lid and select "Slow Cook."
6. Set on Low for 2 hours.
7. Press "Start/Stop" to begin cooking.
8. Place the pan onto a wire rack to cool slightly.

Nutrition

- Calories: 233 g.
- Fat: 19.2 g.
- Net carbohydrates: 6.6 g.
- Carbohydrates: 10.7 g.
- Fiber: 4.1 g.
- Sugar: 5 g.
- Protein: 0.7 g.
- Sodium: 50 mg.

174.   Chocolate Pumpkin Bars

Preparation time: 15 minutes
Cooking time: 3 hours
Servings: 16
Ingredients
For the crust:

- ¾ c. unsweetened coconut, shredded
- ¼ c. cacao powder
- ½ c. raw unsalted sunflower seeds
- ¼ tsp. salt
- ¼ c. Erythritol
- 4 tbsps. butter softened

For the filling:

- 1 (29 oz.) can sugar-free pumpkin puree
- 1 c. heavy cream
- 6 organic eggs
- ½ tsp. salt
- 1 tbsp. organic vanilla extract
- 1 tbsp. pumpkin pie spice
- 1 tsp. cinnamon liquid Stevia
- 1 tsp. Stevia extract

Directions

1. Line the pot of Foodi with a greased parchment paper.
2. **For the crust:** In a food processor, add all the ingredients and pulse until a fine crumbs-like mixture is formed.
3. In the pot prepared of the Foodi, place the crust mixture and press to smooth the top surface.
4. **For the filling:** In the bowl of a stand mixer, add all ingredients and pulse until well combined.
5. Place the filling over crust evenly.
6. Close the Foodi with the Crisping Lid and select "Slow Cook."
7. Set on Low for 3 hours.
8. Press "Start/Stop" to begin cooking.
9. With the help of parchment paper, carefully lift the bars and transfer them onto a wire rack to cool completely.
10. Cut into the desired sizes and serve.

Nutrition

- Calories: 121, Fat: 9.7 g. Carbohydrates: 6.3 g. Fiber: 2.4 g.
- Sugar: 2.2 g. Protein: 3.5 g.

175.   Chocolate Bars

Preparation time: 15 minutes
Cooking time: 2 hours 30 minutes
Servings: 12
Ingredients

- 1 c. Erythritol
- ¼ c. coconut oil, melted
- 1 large organic egg white
- ½ tsp. organic vanilla extract
- 1 ½ c. almond meal
- 1 ¾ tsps. organic baking powder
- ½ tsp. salt
- ½ c. 70% dark chocolate chips
- Almond milk
- Carrots
- Almonds

Directions

1. In the pot of Foodi, place 1 c. of almond milk, carrots, and almonds and stir to combine.
2. Line the pot of Foodi with a greased parchment paper.
3. In a large bowl, add the Erythritol and coconut oil and beat until creamy.
4. Add the egg white and vanilla extract and beat until well combined.
5. Add the almond meal, baking powder, and salt and mix until well combined.
6. Fold in the chocolate chips.
7. In the pot of prepared Foodi, place the mixture and with the back of a spoon, press to smooth the top surface.
8. Close the Foodi with the Crisping Lid and select "Slow Cook."
9. Set on Low for 2–2 ½ hours.
10. Press "Start/Stop" to begin cooking.
11. With a parchment paper, carefully lift the bars and transfer them onto a wire rack to cool completely.
12. Cut into the desired sizes and serve.

Nutrition

- Calories: 177
- Fat: 15.8 g.
- Carbohydrates: 5.6 g.
- Fiber: 2.8 g.
- Sugar: 0.5 g.
- Protein: 4.1 g.

176. Chocolate Fudge 2

Preparation time: 15 minutes
Cooking time: 2 hours
Servings: 30
Ingredients

- 2 ½ c. 70% dark chocolate chips
- ⅓ c. unsweetened coconut milk
- 2 tsps. liquid Stevia
- 1 tsp. organic vanilla extract
- 1 pinch of salt

Directions

1. Lightly, grease the pot of Foodi.
2. In a bowl, add all the ingredients and mix until well combined.
3. In the prepared pot of Foodi, place the mixture evenly.
4. Close the Foodi with the Crisping Lid and select "Slow Cook."
5. Set on Low for 2 hours.
6. Press "Start/Stop" to begin cooking.
7. Now, stir the mixture for about 5 minutes or until smooth.
8. Transfer the mixture into a parchment paper-lined baking sheet and with the back of a spoon, smooth the top surface.
9. Refrigerate to chill for about 30 minutes or until firm.
10. Cut into desired sized squares and serve.

Nutrition

- Calories: 207
- Fat: 16.6 g.
- Carbohydrates: 8.1 g.
- Fiber: 4 g.
- Sugar: 0.1 g.
- Protein: 4.1 g.

177. Cranberry Muffins

Preparation time: 15 minutes
Cooking time: 15 minutes
Servings: 8
Ingredients

- ¼ c. unsweetened almond milk
- 2 large organic eggs
- ½ tsp. organic vanilla extract
- 1 ½ c. almond flour
- ¼ c. Erythritol
- 1 tsp. organic baking powder
- ¼ tsp. ground cinnamon
- ⅛ tsp. salt
- ½ c. fresh cranberries
- ¼ c. walnuts, chopped

Directions

1. In a blender, add the almond milk, eggs, and vanilla extract and pulse for about 20–30 seconds.
2. Add the almond flour, Erythritol, baking powder, cinnamon, and salt and pulse for about 30–45 seconds until well blended.
3. Transfer the mixture into a bowl.
4. Gently, fold in half of the cranberries and walnuts.
5. Place the mixture into 8 silicone muffin cups and top each with remaining cranberries.
6. Arrange the "Cook & Crisp Basket" in the pot of Foodi.
7. Close the Foodi with the Crisping Lid and select "Air Crisp."
8. Set the temperature to 325°F for 5 minutes.
9. Press "Start/Stop" to begin preheating.
10. After preheating, open the lid.
11. Place the ramekins into the "Cook & Crisp Basket."
12. Close the Foodi with the Crisping Lid and select "Air Crisp."
13. Set the temperature to 325°F for 15 minutes.
14. Press "Start/Stop" to begin cooking.
15. Place the muffin cups onto a wire rack to cool completely before serving.

Nutrition

- Calories: 169
- Fat: 14.2 g.
- Carbohydrates: 6.1 g.
- Fiber: 2.9 g.
- Sugar: 1.2 g.
- Protein: 7 g.

178.   Mini Brownie Cakes

Preparation time: 15 minutes
Cooking time: 10 minutes
Servings: 4
Ingredients

- ⅔ c. 70% dark chocolate chips
- 3 organic eggs
- ⅔ c. Erythritol
- 3 ½ tbsps. almond flour
- 1 tsp. organic vanilla extract

Directions

1. In a microwave-safe bowl, add the chocolate chips and microwave for about 1 minute, stirring after every 20 seconds.
2. Remove from the microwave and set aside.
3. In a large bowl, add the eggs, Erythritol, almond flour, and vanilla extract and beat until well combined.
4. Pour the melted chocolate mixture into the egg mixture and beat until well combined.
5. Place the mixture into lightly grease ramekins about halfway full.
6. In the pot of Foodi, place 1 ¾ c. water.
7. Arrange a Reversible Rack in the pot of Foodi.
8. Place 3 ramekins over the Reversible Rack.
9. Arrange a 2nd Reversible Rack on top.
10. Place the remaining 3 ramekins on top of the 2nd Reversible Rack.
11. Close the Foodi with the Pressure Lid and place the pressure valve into a "Seal" position.
12. Select "Pressure" and set it to High for 9 minutes.
13. Press "Start/Stop" to begin cooking.
14. Switch the valve to "Vent" and do a quick release.
15. Place the ramekins onto a wire rack to cool for about 10 minutes.
16. Serve warm.

Nutrition

- Calories: 377
- Fat: 30.5 g.
- Carbohydrates: 11 g.
- Fiber: 6 g.
- Sugar: 0.6 g.
- Protein: 10.8 g.

179.   Mini Chocolate Cakes

Preparation time: 15 minutes
Cooking time: 9 minutes
Servings: 2
Ingredients

- 2 large organic eggs
- 2 tbsps. Erythritol
- 2 tbsps. heavy cream
- ¼ c. cacao powder
- ½ tsp. organic baking powder

Directions

1. In a bowl, add eggs, Erythritol, and cream and beat until well combined.
2. Add the cacao powder and baking powder and mix until well combined.
3. Place the mixture into 2 greased ramekins about halfway full.
4. In the pot of Foodi, place 1 c. water.
5. Arrange a Reversible Rack in the pot of Foodi.
6. Place the ramekins over the Reversible Rack.
7. Close the Foodi with the Pressure Lid and place the pressure valve into a "Seal" position.
8. Select "Pressure" and set it to High for 9 minutes. Press "Start/Stop" to begin cooking.
9. Switch the valve to "Vent" and do a quick release. Place the ramekins onto a wire rack to cool for about 10 minutes. Serve warm.

Nutrition

- Calories: 154
- Fat: 12.5 g.
- Carbohydrates: 8.4 g.
- Fiber: 3 g.
- Sugar: 0.4 g.
- Protein: 8.6 g.

180. Chocolate Lava Cake

Preparation time: 10 minutes
Cooking time: 9 minutes
Servings: 2
Ingredients

- 1 organic egg
- 2 tbsps. cacao powder
- 1 tbsp. golden flax meal
- 2 tbsps. Erythritol
- 1 /8 tsp. Stevia powder
- 2 tbsps. water
- 1 tbsp. coconut oil, melted
- ½ tsp. organic baking powder
- Dash of organic vanilla extract
- 1 pinch of salt

Directions

1. Arrange the "Cook & Crisp Basket" in the pot of Foodi.
2. Close the Foodi with the Crisping Lid and select "Air Crisp."
3. Set the temperature to 350°F for 5 minutes.
4. Press "Start/Stop" to begin preheating.
5. In a small glass Pyrex dish, place all the ingredients and beat until well combined.
6. After preheating, open the lid.
7. Place the Pyrex dish into the "Cook & Crisp Basket."
8. Close the Foodi with the Crisping Lid and select "Air Crisp."
9. Set the temperature to 350°F for 9 minutes.
10. Press "Start/Stop" to begin cooking.
11. Place the ramekins onto a wire rack to cool for about 10 minutes.
12. Serve warm.

Nutrition

- Calories: 120
- Fat: 11.3 g.
- Carbohydrates: 4.3 g.
- Fiber: 2.5 g.
- Sugar: 0.2 g.
- Protein: 4.5 g.

181.   Pumpkin Cake

Preparation time: 15 minutes
Cooking time: 3 hours
Servings: 10
Ingredients

- 1 ½ c. raw pecans
- ¾ c. Erythritol
- ⅓ c. coconut flour
- ¼ c. unflavored whey protein powder
- 2 tsps. organic baking powder
- 1 ½ tsps. ground cinnamon
- 1 tsp. ground ginger
- ¼ tsp. ground cloves
- ¼ tsp. salt
- 4 large organic eggs
- 1 c. pumpkin puree
- ¼ c. butter, melted
- 1 tsp. organic vanilla extract

Directions

1. Grease the pot of Foodi.
2. In a food processor, add the pecans and pulse until they resemble a coarse meal.
3. Transfer the pecans into a bowl.
4. Add the Erythritol, coconut flour, whey protein powder, baking powder, spices, and salt and mix well.
5. Add the eggs, pumpkin puree, butter, and vanilla extract and mix until well combined.
6. Place the mixture into the prepared pot of Foodi evenly.
7. Close the Foodi with the Crisping Lid and select "Slow Cook."
8. Set on Low for 2 ½-3 hours.
9. Press "Start/Stop" to begin cooking.
10. Transfer the pan onto a wire rack to cool for about 10 minutes.
11. Carefully invert the cake onto the wire rack to cool completely.
12. Cut into desired-sized slices and serve.

Nutrition

- Calories: 226
- Fat: 20.2 g.
- Carbohydrates: 6.2 g.
- Fiber: 3.1 g.
- Sugar: 1.7 g.
- Protein: 7.8 g.

182.   Carrot and Coconut Cake

Preparation time: 15 minutes
Cooking time: 3 hours 30 minutes
Servings: 2
Ingredients
For the cake:

- 1 ½ c. almond flour
- ¾ c. Erythritol
- ½ c. walnuts, chopped
- ½ c. unsweetened coconut, shredded
- ¼ c. unsweetened protein powder
- 2 tsps. organic baking powder
- 1 tsp. ground cinnamon
- ¼ tsp. salt
- 4 large organic eggs
- ¼ c. butter, melted
- 3 tbsps. unsweetened almond milk
- ½ tsp. organic vanilla extract
- 2 c. carrots, peeled and grated

For the frosting:

- 6 oz. cream cheese, softened - ½ c. powdered Erythritol
- ½ c. heavy cream
- ¾ tsp. organic vanilla extract

Directions

1. Line the pot of Foodi with a greased parchment paper.
2. **For the cake:** In a large bowl, add the flour, Erythritol, walnuts, coconut, protein powder, baking powder, cinnamon, and salt. Add the remaining ingredients except for carrots and beat until well combined.
3. Fold in the carrots. Place the cake mixture in the prepared pot of Foodi evenly.
4. Close the Foodi with the Crisping Lid and select "Slow Cook."
5. Set on Low for 3–3 ½ hours. Press "Start/Stop" to begin cooking.
6. Transfer the pan onto a wire rack to cool for about 10 minutes.
7. Carefully invert the cake onto the wire rack to cool completely before frosting.
8. **For the frosting:** In a bowl, add the cream cheese and Erythritol and beat until smooth.
9. Add the heavy cream and vanilla extract and beat until well combined.
10. Spread frosting over cooled cake and serve.

Nutrition

- Calories: 269 Fat: 23.6 g. Carbohydrates: 7.1 g. Fiber: 2.7 g. Sugar: 1.9 g.
- Protein: 10 g.

183.   Mini Apple Pies

Preparation time: 10 minutes
Cooking time: 25 minutes
Servings: 6
Ingredients

- 8 tbsp. butter, softened
- 12 tbsp. brown sugar
- 2 tsp. cinnamon, ground
- 4 medium Granny Smith apples, diced
- 2 tsp. cornstarch
- 4 tsp. cold water
- 1 (14 oz) package pastry, 9-inch crust pie
- Cooking spray
- ½ c. powdered sugar
- 2 tsp. milk

Directions

1. Toss apples, with brown sugar, butter, and cinnamon in a suitable skillet.
2. Place the skillet over medium heat and stir-cook for 5 minutes.
3. Mix cornstarch with cold water in a small bowl.
4. Add cornstarch mixture into the apple and cook for 1 minute until it thickens.
5. Remove this filling from the heat and allow it to cool.
6. Unroll the pie crust and spray on a floured surface.
7. Cut the dough into 16 equal rectangles.
8. Wet the edges of the 8 rectangles with water and divide the apple filling at the center of these rectangles.
9. Place the other 8 rectangles on top and crimp the edges with a fork.
10. Place 4 small pies in each of the Air Fryer baskets.
11. Return the Air Fryer baskets to the Air Fryer.
12. Select the "Air Fryer" mode for Zone 1 with 390°F temperature and 17 minutes cooking time.
13. Press the "Match Cook" button to copy the settings for Zone 2.
14. Start cooking by pressing the "Start/Pause" button.
15. Flip the pies once cooked halfway through, and resume cooking.
16. Meanwhile, mix sugar with milk.
17. Pour this mixture over the apple pies.
18. Serve fresh.

Nutrition

- Calories: 271 Total fat: 15 g.
- Saturated fat: 7 g. Cholesterol: 46 mg. Sodium: 178 mg.
- Total carbohydrates: 33 g. Fiber: 1 g.Sugar: 26 g. Protein: 4 g.

184.　　Walnuts Fritters

Preparation time: 10 minutes
Cooking time: 15 minutes
Servings: 8
Ingredients

- Cooking spray
- 1 c. all-purpose flour
- ½ c. walnuts, coarsely chopped
- ¼ c. white sugar
- ¼ c. milk
- 1 egg
- 1 ½ tsp. baking powder
- 1 pinch salt
- 2 tbsp. white sugar
- ½ tsp. ground cinnamon

For the glaze:

- ½ c. confectioners' sugar
- 1 tbsp. milk
- ½ tsp. caramel extract
- ¼ tsp. ground cinnamon

Directions

1. Layer both Air Fryer baskets with parchment paper.
2. Grease the parchment paper with cooking spray.
3. Whisk flour with milk, ¼ c. sugar, egg, baking powder, and salt in a small bowl.
4. Separately mix 2 tbsp. sugar with cinnamon in another bowl, toss in walnuts, and mix well to coat.
5. Stir in flour mixture and mix until combined.
6. Drop the fritters mixture using a cookie scoop into the 2 Air Fryer baskets.
7. Return the Air Fryer baskets to the Air Fryer.
8. Select the "Air Fryer" mode for Zone 1 with 375°F temperature and 15 minutes cooking time.
9. Press the "Match Cook" button to copy the settings for Zone 2.
10. Start cooking by pressing the "Start/Pause" button.
11. Flip the fritters once cooked halfway through, then resume cooking.
12. Meanwhile, whisk milk, caramel extract, confectioners' sugar, and cinnamon in a bowl.
13. Transfer fritters to a wire rack and allow them to cool.
14. Drizzle the fritters with the glaze.

Nutrition

- Calories: 146 Total fat: 5 g. Saturated fat: 7 g. Cholesterol: 46 mg. Sodium: 145 mg.
- Total carbohydrates: 16 g. Fiber: 1 g. Sugar: 13 g. Protein: 6 g.

185.   Air Fried Bananas

Preparation time: 10 minutes
Cooking time: 13 minutes
Servings: 4
Ingredients

- 4 bananas, sliced into ⅛-inch-thick diagonals
- 1 serving avocado oil cooking spray

Directions

1. Spread the banana slices in the 2 Air Fryer baskets in a single layer.
2. Drizzle avocado oil over the banana slices.
3. Return the Air Fryer baskets to the Air Fryer.
4. Select the "Air Fryer" mode for Zone 1 with 350°F temperature and 13 minutes cooking time.
5. Press the "Match Cook" button to copy the settings for Zone 2.
6. Start cooking by pressing the "Start/Pause" button.
7. Serve.

Nutrition

- Calories: 171
- Total fat: 1 g.
- Saturated fat: 2 g.
- Cholesterol: 6 mg.
- Sodium: 108 mg.
- Total carbohydrates: 23 g.
- Fiber: 1 g.
- Sugar: 6 g.
- Protein: 2 g.

186.   Crispy Beignets

Preparation time: 10 minutes
Cooking time: 17 minutes
Servings: 6
Ingredients

- Cooking spray
- ¼ c. white sugar
- ⅛ c. water
- ½ c. all-purpose flour
- 1 large egg, separated
- 1 ½ tsp. butter, melted
- ½ tsp. baking powder
- ½ tsp. vanilla extract
- 1 pinch salt
- 2 tbsp. confectioners' sugar, or to taste

Directions

1. Beat flour with water, sugar, egg yolk, baking powder, butter, vanilla extract, and salt in a large bowl, until lumps-free.
2. Beat egg whites in a separate bowl and beat using an electric hand mixer until it forms soft peaks.
3. Add the egg white to the flour batter and mix gently until fully incorporated.
4. Divide the dough into small beignets and place them in the Air Fryer baskets.
5. Return the Air Fryer baskets to the Air Fryer.
6. Select the "Air Fryer" mode for Zone 1 with 390°F temperature and 17 minutes cooking time.
7. Press the "Match Cook" button to copy the settings for Zone 2.
8. Start cooking by pressing the "Start/Pause" button.
9. And cook for another 4 minutes. Dust the cooked beignets with sugar.
10. Serve.

Nutrition

- Calories: 212
- Total fat: 8 g.
- Saturated fat: 9 g.
- Cholesterol: 26 mg.
- Sodium: 153 mg.
- Total carbohydrates: 51 g.
- Fiber: 1 g.
- Sugar: 27 g.
- Protein: 3 g.

187.   Cinnamon Doughnuts

Preparation time: 10 minutes
Cooking time: 15 minutes
Servings: 6
Ingredients

- 1 can pre-made biscuit dough
- ½ c. white sugar
- 1 tsp. cinnamon
- ½ c. powdered sugar
- Coconut oil
- Melted butter, to brush biscuits

Directions

1. Place all the biscuits on a cutting board and cut holes in the center of each biscuit using a cookie cutter.
2. Grease the Air Fryer baskets with coconut oil.
3. Place the biscuits in the 2 Air Fryer baskets while keeping them 1-inch apart.
4. Return the Air Fryer baskets to the Air Fryer.
5. Select the "Air Fryer" mode for Zone 1 with 375°F temperature and 15 minutes cooking time.
6. Press the "Match Cook" button to copy the settings for Zone 2.
7. Start cooking by pressing the "Start/Pause" button.
8. Brush all the donuts with melted butter and sprinkle cinnamon and sugar on top.
9. Air fry these donuts for one minute more.
10. Enjoy.

Nutrition

- Calories: 282
- Total fat: 5 g.
- Saturated fat: 12 g.
- Cholesterol: 116 mg.
- Sodium: 10 mg.
- Total carbohydrates: 25 g.
- Fiber: 1 g.
- Sugar: 26 g.
- Protein: 2 g.

188.   Cranberry Scones

Preparation time: 10 minutes
Cooking time: 16 minutes
Servings: 4
Ingredients

- 4 c. flour
- ½ c. brown sugar
- 2 tbsp. baking powder
- ½ tsp. ground nutmeg
- ½ tsp. salt
- 2 c. fresh cranberry
- ⅔ c. sugar
- 2 tbsp. orange zest
- 1 ¼ c. half and half cream
- 2 eggs

Directions

1. Whisk flour with baking powder, salt, nutmeg, and both the sugar in a bowl.
2. Stir in egg and cream, mix well to form a smooth dough.
3. Fold in cranberries along with the orange zest.
4. Knead this dough well on a work surface.
5. Cut 3-inch circles out of the dough.
6. Divide the scones in the Air Fryer baskets and spray them with cooking oil.
7. Return the Air Fryer baskets to the Air Fryer.
8. Select the "Air Fryer" mode for Zone 1 with 375°F temperature and 16 minutes cooking time.
9. Press the "Match Cook" button to copy the settings for Zone 2.
10. Start cooking by pressing the "Start/Pause" button.
11. Flip the scones once cooked halfway and resume cooking.
12. Enjoy.

Nutrition

- Calories: 292
- Total fat: 2 g.
- Saturated fat: 7 g.
- Cholesterol: 46 mg.
- Sodium: 112 mg.
- Total carbohydrates: 41 g.
- Fiber: 1 g.
- Sugar: 26 g.
- Protein: 4 g.

189.   Apple Flautas

Preparation time: 10 minutes
Cooking time: 8 minutes
Servings: 6
Ingredients

- ¼ c. light brown sugar
- ⅛ c. all-purpose flour
- ¼ tsp. ground cinnamon
- Nutmeg, to taste
- 4 apples, peeled, cored and sliced
- ½ lemon, juice, and zest
- 6 (10-inch) flour tortillas
- Vegetable oil
- Caramel sauce
- Cinnamon sugar

Directions

1. Preheat your Air Fryer machine at 400°F.
2. Mix brown sugar with cinnamon, nutmeg, and flour in a large bowl.
3. Toss in apples in lemon juice. Mix well.
4. Place a tortilla at a time on a flat surface and add ½ c. of the apple mixture to the tortilla.
5. Roll the tortilla into a burrito and seal it tightly and hold it in place with a toothpick.
6. Repeat the same steps with the remaining tortillas and apple mixture.
7. Place 2 apple burritos in each of the Air Fryer baskets and spray them with cooking oil.
8. Return the Air Fryer baskets to the Air Fryer.
9. Select the "Air Fryer" mode for Zone 1 with 400°F temperature and 8 minutes cooking time.
10. Press the "Match Cook" button to copy the settings for Zone 2.
11. Start cooking by pressing the "Start/Pause" button.
12. Flip the burritos once cooked halfway through, then resume cooking.
13. Garnish with caramel sauce and cinnamon sugar.
14. Enjoy!

Nutrition

- Calories: 236
- Total fat: 5 g.
- Saturated fat: 3 g.
- Cholesterol: 154 mg.
- Sodium: 113 mg.
- Total carbohydrates: 43 g.
- Fiber: 1 g. Sugar: 26 g.
- Protein: 6 g.

190. Apple Oats Crisp

Preparation time: 10 minutes
Cooking time: 14 minutes
Servings: 6
Ingredients

- 3 c. apples, chopped
- 1 tbsp. pure maple syrup
- 2 tsp. lemon juice
- 3 tbsp. all-purpose flour, divided
- ⅓ c. quick oats
- ¼ c. brown sugar
- 2 tbsp. light butter, melted
- ½ tsp. cinnamon

Directions

1. Toss the chopped apples with 1 tbsp. all-purpose flour, cinnamon, maple syrup, and lemon juice in a suitable bowl.
2. Divide the apples in the 2 Air Fryer baskets with their crisper plates.
3. Whisk oats, brown sugar, and remaining all-purpose flour in a small bowl.
4. Stir in melted butter, then divide this mixture over the apples.
5. Return the Air Fryer baskets to the Air Fryer.
6. Select the "Bake" mode for Zone 1 with 375°F temperature and 14 minutes cooking time.
7. Press the "Match Cook" button to copy the settings for Zone 2.
8. Start cooking by pressing the "Start/Pause" button.
9. Enjoy fresh.

Nutrition

- Calories: 264
- Total fat: 14 g.
- Saturated fat: 9 g.
- Cholesterol: 46 mg.
- Sodium: 117 mg.
- Total carbohydrates: 33 g.
- Fiber: 1 g.
- Sugar: 26 g.
- Protein: 4 g.

191.   Blueberry Lemon Muffins

Preparation time: 5 minutes
Cooking time: 10 minutes
Servings: 12
Ingredients

- 1 tsp. vanilla
- Juice and zest of 1 lemon
- 2 eggs
- 1 c. blueberries
- ½ c. cream
- ¼ c. avocado oil
- ½ c. monk fruit
- 2 ½ c. almond flour

Directions

1. Mix monk fruit and flour together.
2. In another bowl, mix vanilla, egg, lemon juice, zest, and cream together. Add mixtures together and blend well.
3. Spoon batter into cupcake holders.
4. Place in the Air Fryer. Bake 10 minutes at 320°F, checking at 6 minutes to ensure you do not overbake them.

Nutrition

- Calories: 317
- Fat: 11 g.
- Protein: 3 g.
- Sugar: 5 g.

192.   Grilled Pound Cake with Berry Compote

Preparation time: 5 minutes
Cooking time: 30 minutes
Servings: 4
Ingredients
For the pound cake:

- 1 c. butter, softened
- 1 c. sugar
- 4 eggs
- 1 tsp. vanilla
- 1 pinch of salt
- 2 c. flour

Directions

1. Mix the compote ingredients together in a saucepan. Bring to a boil, stirring well. Remove from the heat and set aside.
2. In a mixing bowl, mix the butter and sugar until fluffy.
3. Add the eggs one at a time, mixing well between each egg.
4. Add the vanilla and salt.
5. Stir in the flour until well combined, but do not overmix.
6. Scoop and level the pound cake batter out onto a sheet pan.
7. Bake until the cake is golden brown.
8. Once the pound cake is cooled, cut into 3-inch squares.
9. Heat the Grill Grate to medium and grill the pound cakes lightly. Serve warm with the compote drizzled over the top.

Nutrition

- Calories: 317
- Fat: 11 g.
- Protein: 3 g.
- Sugar: 5 g.

193. Sweet Cream Cheese Wontons

Preparation time: 5 minutes
Cooking time: 5 minutes
Servings: 16
Ingredients

- 1 egg mixed with a bit of water
- Wonton wrappers
- ½ c. powdered Erythritol
- 8 oz. softened cream cheese
- Olive oil

Directions

1. Mix sweetener and cream cheese together.
2. Lay out 4 wontons at a time and cover with a dish towel to prevent drying out.
3. Place ½ of a tsp. cream cheese mixture into each wrapper.
4. Dip finger into egg/water mixture and fold diagonally to form a triangle. Seal edges well.
5. Repeat with remaining ingredients.
6. Insert the Crisper Basket and close the hood. Select "Air Crisp," set the temperature to 400°F, and set the time to 5 minutes. Select "Start/Stop" to begin preheating.
7. Air frying. Place filled wontons into the Air Fryer and cook 5 minutes at 400°F, shaking halfway through cooking.

Nutrition

- Calories: 303
- Fat: 3 g.
- Protein: 1 g.
- Sugar: 4 g.

194.   Air Fryer Cinnamon Rolls

Preparation time: 15 minutes
Cooking time: 5 minutes
Servings: 8
Ingredients

- 1 ½ tbsp. cinnamon
- ¾ c. brown sugar
- ¼ c. melted coconut oil
- 1 lb. frozen bread dough, thawed

Directions

1. Lay out bread dough and roll it out into a rectangle. Brush coconut oil over the dough and leave a 1-inch border along the edges.
2. Mix cinnamon and sweetener together and then sprinkle over dough.
3. Roll dough tightly and slice into 8 pieces. Let sit 1–2 hours to rise.
4. To make the glaze, simply mix ingredients together till smooth.
5. Once rolls rise, place into the Air Fryer and cook for 5 minutes at 350°F.
6. Serve rolls drizzled in cream cheese glaze. Enjoy!

Nutrition

- Calories: 390
- Fat: 8 g.
- Protein: 1 g.
- Sugar: 7 g.

195.   Smoked Apple Crumble

Preparation time: 5 minutes
Cooking time: 45 minutes
Servings: 4
Ingredients

- Brown sugar
- Flour
- Oatmeal
- Caramel chips
- Pecans
- Cinnamon
- Baking powder
- Salt
- Cold butter
- 1-2 pecan wood chunks
- French vanilla ice cream

For the filling:

- 4–5 large Honeycrisp apples, peeled and sliced
- Juice from ½ lemon
- 2 tbsp. flour
- ⅓ c. sugar
- 1 tbsp. ground cinnamon
- 1 tsp. ground nutmeg

Directions

1. Insert the Grill Grate and close the hood. Select "Grill," set the temperature to High, and set the time to 40 minutes. Select "Start/Stop" to begin preheating.
2. Place apples in a large mixing bowl and toss with lemon juice. Then add in flour, sugar, cinnamon, and nutmeg, and mix thoroughly.
3. Pour apples into a greased cast-iron pan. Set mixture aside.
4. Using the now-empty mixing bowl, combine brown sugar, flour, oatmeal, caramel chips, pecans, cinnamon, baking powder, and salt for the topping.
5. Using a pastry blender or large fork, cut the cold butter into the topping mix.
6. Cover apples with the topping mixture.
7. Add 1–2 pecan wood chunks to the hot coals. Place apple crumble over the roasting rack.
8. Close the hood and bake until apples start to bubble, and the topping begins to brown (about 45 minutes).
9. Remove from the grill and serve warm with French vanilla ice cream.

Nutrition

- Calories: 317 Fat: 11 g. Protein: 3 g. Sugar: 5 g.

196.   Bread Pudding With Cranberry

Preparation time: 5 minutes
Cooking time: 35 minutes
Servings: 4
Ingredients

- 2 ½ eggs
- ½ c. cranberries
- ¼ c. and 2 tbsps. white sugar
- ¼ c. golden raisins
- ⅛ tsp. ground cinnamon
- ¾ c. heavy whipping cream
- ¾ tsp. lemon zest
- ¾ tsp. kosher salt
- ¾ French baguettes, cut into 2-inch slices
- ⅜ vanilla bean, split and seeds scraped away

Directions

1. Lightly grease the baking pan of the Air Fryer with cooking spray. Spread baguette slices, cranberries, and raisins.
2. In a blender, blend well vanilla bean, cinnamon, salt, lemon zest, eggs, sugar, and cream. Pour over baguette slices. Let it soak for 1 hour.
3. Cover pan with foil.
4. For 35 minutes, cook at 330°F.
5. Let it rest for 10 minutes. Serve and enjoy!

Nutrition

- Calories: 590
- Fat: 25 g.
- Protein: 17 g.
- Sugar: 9 g.

197.   Black and White Brownies

Preparation time: 10 minutes
Cooking time: 20 minutes
Servings: 8
Ingredients

- 1 egg
- ¼ c. brown sugar
- 2 tbsps. white sugar
- 2 tbsps. safflower oil
- 1 tsp. vanilla
- ¼ c. cocoa powder
- ⅓ c. all-purpose flour
- ¼ c. white chocolate chips
- Nonstick baking spray with flour

Directions

1. In a medium bowl, beat the egg with the brown sugar and the white sugar. Beat in the oil and the vanilla.
2. Add the cocoa powder and flour and stir just until combined. Fold in the white chocolate chips.
3. Spray a 6x6x2-inch baking pan with nonstick spray. Spoon the brownie batter into the pan.
4. Bake for 20 minutes or until the brownies are set when lightly touched with a finger. Let cool for 30 minutes before slicing to serve.

Nutrition

- Calories: 317
- Fat: 11 g.
- Protein: 3 g.
- Sugar: 5 g.

198.   French Toast Bites

Preparation time: 5 minutes
Cooking time: 15 minutes
Servings: 8
Ingredients

- Almond milk
- Cinnamon
- Sweetener
- 3 eggs
- 4 pieces wheat bread

Directions

1. Insert the Crisper Basket and close the hood. Select "Air Crisp," set the temperature to 360°F, and set the time to 15 minutes. Select "Start/Stop" to begin preheating.
2. Whisk eggs and thin out with almond milk.
3. Mix ⅓ c. of sweetener with lots of cinnamon.
4. Tear bread in half, ball up pieces, and press together to form a ball.
5. Soak bread balls in egg and then roll into cinnamon sugar, making sure to thoroughly coat.
6. Place coated bread balls into the Air Fryer and bake for 15 minutes.

Nutrition

- Calories: 300
- Fat: 10 g.
- Protein: 2 g.
- Sugar: 4 g.

199.   Baked Apple

Preparation time: 5 minutes
Cooking time: 20 minutes
Servings: 4
Ingredients

- ¼ c. water
- ¼ tsp. nutmeg
- ¼ tsp. cinnamon
- 1 ½ tsp. melted ghee
- 2 tbsp. raisins
- 2 tbsp. chopped walnuts
- 1 medium apple

Directions

1. Insert the Crisper Basket and close the hood. Select "Air Crisp," set the temperature to 350°F, and set the time to 20 minutes. Select "Start/Stop" to begin preheating.
2. Slice the apple in half and discard some of the flesh from the center.
3. Place into the frying pan.
4. Mix remaining ingredients together except water. Spoon mixture to the middle of apple halves.
5. Pour water over the filled apples.
6. Place pan with apple halves into the Air Fryer, bake for 20 minutes.

Nutrition

- Calories: 205
- Fat: 11 g.
- Protein: 2 g.
- Sugar: 5 g.

200.   Coffee and Blueberry Cake

Preparation time: 5 minutes
Cooking time: 35 minutes
Servings: 6
Ingredients

- 1 c. white sugar
- 1 egg
- ½ c. butter softened
- ½ c. fresh or frozen blueberries
- ½ c. sour cream
- ½ tsp. baking powder
- ½ tsp. ground cinnamon
- ½ tsp. vanilla extract
- ¼ c. brown sugar
- ¼ c. chopped pecans
- ⅛ tsp. salt
- 1 ½ tsps. confectioners' sugar for dusting
- ¾ c. all-purpose flour, plus 1 tbsp.

Directions

1. In a small bowl, whisk well pecans, cinnamon, and brown sugar.
2. In a blender, blend well all the wet ingredients. Add the dry ingredients, except for the confectioner's sugar and the blueberries. Blend well until smooth and creamy.
3. Lightly grease baking pan of Air Fryer with cooking spray.
4. Pour half of the batter into the pan. Sprinkle half of the pecan mixture on top. Pour the remaining batter. And then topped with the remaining pecan mixture.
5. Cover pan with foil.
6. For 35 minutes, cook at 330°F.
7. Serve and enjoy with a dusting of confectioner's sugar.

Nutrition

- Calories: 480
- Fat: 26 g.
- Protein: 5 g.
- Sugar: 8 g.

201.   Cinnamon Sugar Roasted Chickpeas

Preparation time: 5 minutes
Cooking time: 10 minutes
Servings: 2
Ingredients

- 1 tbsp. sweetener
- 1 tbsp. cinnamon
- 1 c. chickpeas

Directions

1. Insert the Crisper Basket and close the hood. Select "Air Crisp," set the temperature to 390°F, and set the time to 10 minutes. Select "Start/Stop" to begin preheating.
2. Rinse and drain chickpeas.
3. Mix all ingredients together and add to the Air Fryer.
4. Cook for 10 minutes.

Nutrition

- Calories: 115
- Fat: 20 g.
- Protein: 18 g.
- Sugar: 7 g.

202.   Cherry-Choco Bars

Preparation time: 5 minutes
Cooking time: 15 minutes
Servings: 8
Ingredients

- ¼ tsp. salt
- ½ c. almonds, sliced
- ½ c. chia seeds
- ½ c. dark chocolate, chopped
- ½ c. dried cherries, chopped
- ½ c. prunes, pureed
- ½ c. quinoa, cooked
- ¾ c. almond butter
- ⅓ c. honey
- 2 c. old-fashioned oats
- 2 tbsp. coconut oil

Directions

1. Insert the Crisper Basket and close the hood. Select "Air Crisp," set the temperature to 375°F, and set the time to 15 minutes. Select "Start/Stop" to begin preheating.
2. In a mixing bowl, combine the oats, quinoa, chia seeds, almond, cherries, and chocolate.
3. In a saucepan, heat the almond butter, honey, and coconut oil.
4. Pour the butter mixture over the dry mixture. Add salt and prunes.
5. Mix until well combined.
6. Pour over a baking dish that can fit inside the Air Fryer.
7. Cook for 15 minutes.
8. Let it cool for an hour before slicing into bars.

Nutrition

- Calories: 330
- Fat: 15 g.
- Protein: 7 g.
- Sugar: 8 g.

203.   Cinnamon Fried Bananas

Preparation time: 5 minutes
Cooking time: 10 minutes
Servings: 2–3
Ingredients

- 1 c. panko breadcrumbs
- 3 tbsp. cinnamon
- ½ c. almond flour
- 3 egg whites
- 8 ripe bananas
- 3 tbsp. vegan coconut oil

Directions

1. Heat the coconut oil and add the breadcrumbs. Mix around 2–3 minutes until golden. Pour into a bowl.
2. Peel and cut the bananas in half. Roll the half of each banana into flour, eggs, cinnamon, and crumb mixture.
3. Place into the Air Fryer. Cook for 10 minutes at 280°F.
4. A great addition to a healthy banana split!

Nutrition

- Calories: 215
- Fat: 11 g.
- Protein: 5 g.
- Sugar: 5 g.

Conclusion

The Foodi 2-Basket Air Fryer is an awesome way to cook and fry food without all the added calories. The basket on the bottom of the Air Fryer has 2 compartments: one for cooking and one for warming. The Foodi 2-Basket Air Fryer is an awesome device that has the ability to cook with little to no oil. This is great for those who want to eat healthy and yet get the delicious fried taste that they crave.

The main aim of the Foodi is to make your cooking life as simple and hassle-free as possible. For instance, just like with a slow cooker, you can leave your meal to cook overnight, and then when you wake up in the morning, it's ready for you to eat. What's wonderful is that you don't need to think about the meal overcooking while you're sleeping. If you set your food to cook for 8 hours, it will automatically shut off after that time and remain warm for several hours.

It's about time that you give these 2-Basket Air Fryer recipes a try and surprise your family and loved ones with their great flavor and super crispy texture. In this cookbook, we have tried to introduce you to the recent hit of the air frying technology, the Foodi 2-Basket Air Fryer, and brought you all the basic and easy-to-start-with recipes that will help you create a complete menu of your own.

The 2-Basket Air Fryer has come as an amazing surprise for all those who always wanted to cook a variety of meals at the time and save some time. Now with this Air Fryer, a person can use 2 different chambers at a time—each of them having a 4-quart volume for cooking. Or a user can simply sync them together to get an 8-quart capacity. Isn't that amazing? Now cooking large and small serving portions is not a problem as long as you have this Air Fryer at home.

Foodi, due to its effective dual chamber heating technology and amazing design, has upgraded the air frying landscape, and it is now giving major competition to all its Air Fryer competitors in the market. Not only this Air Fryer provides 2 chambers to cook as much food as you want to cook, but it is extremely user-friendly as well. You can sync the 2 baskets to cook at the same time and temperature, or you can use them as separate independent chambers to cook different meals at the same time.

So, if you haven't yet tried the 2-Basket Air Fryer or are still getting a grasp at this technology, then this cookbook is the right fit for you! You have all the luscious meals to prepare all sorts of meat cuts, vegetarian entrees, snacks, desserts, and breakfast in just a few minutes. So, don't wait around; put on your aprons, pick your favorite recipe from this book, and do some air frying today!

Printed in Great Britain
by Amazon